Communicative
Sexualities

Communicative Sexualities

A Communicology of Sexual Experience

Jacqueline M. Martinez

LEXINGTON BOOKS
Lanham • Boulder • New York • Toronto • Plymouth, UK

Published by Lexington Books
A wholly owned subsidiary of The Rowman & Littlefield Publishing Group, Inc.
4501 Forbes Boulevard, Suite 200, Lanham, Maryland 20706
www.lexingtonbooks.com

Estover Road, Plymouth PL6 7PY, United Kingdom

British Library Cataloguing in Publication Information Available

Library of Congress Cataloging-in-Publication Data

Martinez, Jacqueline M., 1961–
  Communicative sexualities : a communicology of sexual experience / Jacqueline
M. Martinez.
      p. cm.
  Includes bibliographical references and index.
  ISBN 978-0-7391-2535-9 (cloth : alk. paper)—ISBN 978-0-7391-2536-6 (pbk. :
alk. paper)—ISBN 978-0-7391-4802-0 (ebook)
  1. Sexology—Research. 2. Semiotics. 3. Communication. 4. Phenomenology.
5. Queer theory. 6. Feminist theory. I. Title.
  HQ60.M37 2011
  305.4201—dc22
                                                          2011008117

∞™ The paper used in this publication meets the minimum requirements of
American National Standard for Information Sciences—Permanence of Paper
for Printed Library Materials, ANSI/NISO Z39.48-1992.

Printed in the United States of America

To Lisa, Jerri, and Barbara,
the best and most loving
support team ever

Contents

List of Figures   ix

List of Tables   xi

Acknowledgments   xiii

Preface   xv

1 An Introduction to Sexuality as Subject Matter   1

2 Our Lived-Experience of Sexuality as the Subject of Research   17

3 History, Time, Context   43

4 Semiotics in Communicology   57

5 Phenomenology in Communicology   71

6 Semiotic Phenomenology   97

7 Semiotic Phenomenology Applied   113

8 Cultural Ethics and Personal Obligations   127

Works Cited   137

Index   139

About the Author   143

List of Figures

4.1 Paradigmatic and Syntagmatic Axes of Language   66

6.1 Theory and Methodology of Semiotic Phenomenology   102

6.2 Lanigan's Comparative Research Procedure Involving the
Order of Experience (OE) and the Order of Analysis (OA)   105

6.3 Ihde's Phenomenological Process   108

List of Tables

4.1   Paradigmatic and Syntagmatic Choices   67

5.1   Information Theory versus Communication Theory   92

7.1   List of Possible Topics Related to Sexuality   115

Acknowledgments

Without Richard Lanigan, his work, his mentoring, and friendship, I would never have found the passion and love I have in studying and teaching communicology. Richard's presence as a scholar of tremendous accomplishment, and his compassion and understanding as a friend, have been central in all that I have been able to achieve in my career. I am eternally grateful. My communicology colleagues have provided a rich and engaging community that has been crucial in my own intellectual and scholarly growth. Maureen Connolly and Tom Craig have been especially important in this regard.

Over the past ten years or so, I have benefited from the dialogue, critical engagement, and friendship of many colleagues whose sharp minds and quick wits have inspired and helped sustain me. Most important among these colleagues are Tom Nakayama and Judith Martin. I thank them both for sharing their intellect and friendship with me, and for being there through some difficult times. I also enjoy support from Frederick Corey and Barbara Lafford, colleagues at Arizona State University who created an institutional environment in which I could pursue the work presented here. I thank Lisa Anderson and Barbara Klein for reading the early drafts of this work pretty much immediately as they came out of my printer, and Richard Lanigan for reading the first completed draft of the book. The feedback from each of them was invaluable. I thank Lenore Lautigar and the people at Lexington Books for their support of this project, and for their professional and efficient manner in seeing it through the production and publication process.

I need to thank every student I have had in my Communicative Sexualities course over the past several years at Arizona State University. Their willingness to respond to my challenges, and to trust my own ability to cultivate and maintain a safe, mature, and respectful environment in which they could look directly and collectively at their lived, immediate, and concrete experiences of sexuality, has taught me more than I ever could have learned otherwise. They have affirmed for me over and over again my initial sense that young people today are very capable of rising to the challenge of examining their personal experiences of sexuality despite living in a culture that generally discourages that. I especially thank Brandon Ferderer, Jennifer Hackney, and Jeremy Omori, each of whom took the course and then returned to assist me in subsequent classes.

On a very personal level, I could not have completed the work presented here were it not for support, care, and love offered me by Lisa Anderson, my life-partner; Jerrilene Martinez, my identical twin sister; and Barbara Klein, a new friend who has made all the difference. My sense of gratitude to each of them is beyond my ability to express in words—I know because I have tried. I am deeply, deeply grateful. This book is dedicated to them.

Preface

I have approached the process of writing this text as a *teacher*—as a college professor whose primary objective is, simply, to reach students in ways that matter. In this sense, I am not unlike what I believe are the vast majority of teachers who find their professional purpose and direction in the desire to make a difference in young people's lives. I am more fortunate than most, however, in that my experience, education, and training have provided me with particular insights and understanding that have allowed me to achieve the practical results detailed in this text and, more importantly, in my own and the lives of the two hundred or so students whom I have had in my Communicative Sexualities course over the past several years. This book is the result of my having worked with each of these students in a collective effort to systematically study our sexual experience in direct, immediate, and thoroughgoing ways.

Issues related to sexuality have played an important role in virtually every aspect of my life experience, education, and training. Indeed, it was the recognition of my sexual desire for other women, at around the age of twenty-two, that propelled me into a life dedicated to intellectual endeavors. It was recognition of being gay that brought the totality of my life up to that moment into an entirely different view. Suddenly, my internal sense of self took on a resonance that allowed me, simply, to recognize myself. I recognized myself in ways that reverberated through every aspect of my self-knowledge. At that moment of "coming out," the entirety of my life made sense in ways it simply hadn't the moment before.

At that moment of "coming out," I also knew that this profoundly new and resonant sense of self-understanding had to remain completely hidden from everyone in my life. I did not share the incredible sense of growth and joyousness that came with those first expressions of a sexuality that I had not recognized previously. I continued in my life as if nothing had changed. But, of course, everything had changed. Because I was raised in an all-encompassing heteronormativity, there was simply no context within which I could talk with anyone about my self-discoveries. I began to seek out other people who I thought might also be gay, and I began to read voraciously everything I could about lesbianism, homosexuality, feminism, culture, and so on. Had it not been for the many deeply relevant questions I came to have about myself, my family, community, and social environment, I would never have considered pursuing a graduate education.

The single most important aspect of my graduate training was its focus on *communication* as the immediate, concrete, and embodied means through which all things human become possible. My training in communicology and its methodological practice of semiotic phenomenology was intense and demanding. I recognized, early on, that what I was studying addressed some of the most challenging intellectual and practical problems of our day. I also recognized that it would take many years to master, and that to actually achieve the scholarly and human success I was seeking would require a continuous and long-term commitment far surpassing my days as a graduate student. The words of Edmund Husserl comforted me: the phenomenologist is a "perpetual beginner." Thus, I was able to take my abiding interest in understanding the fact of lived-experience, alongside my continued study of communicology and semiotic phenomenology, as, basically, the shorthand version of my entire scholarly and teaching career.

I emphasize my own background and experience because I think it is helpful for the reader to have a sense of how I have come to think and teach the way I do about sexuality, communication, and issues related to identity and prejudice generally. My first intellectual passions centered around the feminist movement as developed by both academic and non-academic writers. I began my intellectual career as a committed feminist and have remained so ever since. As an academic feminist coming of age during the late 1980s and early 1990s, I was engaged in what I think are some of the most important movements in intellectual and scholarly work of the last half of the twentieth century and this first decade of the twenty-first century. Highlights of these movements include the classic conflicts between center and periphery. Early on, U.S. American feminist theory posited the "center" as dominated by "white males" and the many scholarly canons that claimed to represent the highest achievements of a culture while systematically excluding the contributions, perspectives, and experiences of women. Women, and women's experience, therefore became the "periphery" from which new, more accurate, and insightful accounts of human culture and practices could be known. It did not take long, however, for the best feminist theorists of the day—many of them women of color—to critique the use of the male-center/women-periphery as a basis for genuine insight and understanding regarding the prejudices, discriminations, and ignorance that circulated so freely within our social world. This contested ground of intellectual work was driven by the insistence that attention be directed to the concrete circumstances of people's lives across cultural, social, and economic categories of all sorts, and led to what has become a touchstone of much of our contemporary social thought—the intersections of race-class-gender.

The focus on the intersections of race-class-gender within the United States coincided with a growing interest in European philosophical traditions, particularly those we refer to as postmodernism, poststructuralism, and deconstruction. Feminist critiques of, and engagement with, these traditions account for the emergence of what became known as queer theory. It was with the development of queer theory that our basic notions of identity as singular, stable, and accurate accounts of human embodiment were most strongly critiqued. These intellectual movements have occupied much of my scholarly career and are detailed in my earlier work, *Phenomenology of Chicana Experience and Identity: Communication and Transformation in Praxis* (Rowman & Littlefield, 2000). See also Martinez (2003, 2006, 2008).

When I first began conceptualizing what has become the present work, I had in mind a detailing of the philosophical, theoretical, and practical intersections between these movements in feminist theory, queer theory, and the development of communicology and semiotic phenomenology. But, I simply could not make that happen because my attention was occupied by the very specific demands and responsibilities of teaching a course on sexuality structured around a direct, sustained, and thoroughgoing examination of sexuality as we experience it in the immediacy of our concrete practices—that is, in our lived-body. In the end, the most important theoretical accomplishments turned out to be those driven by a constant concern with the embodied realities engaged and developed in the classroom as we applied the research procedures of semiotic phenomenology. The very specific and distinct intricacies of the intersections wherein theory entails practice, and practice entails theory, became more clear and concrete as we grappled with and successfully applied the procedures of semiotic phenomenology.

Over the past several years of teaching Communicative Sexualities, I have become very aware of the importance of the difference between theory and practice, especially in the academy and among those of us who posit our teaching efforts as in some sense expanding students' consciousness—a project that I think is essential to education. I have come to discover just how challenging it is to maintain clarity regarding the difference between the unique insights I bring to the classroom and the insightfulness I hope the students will discover for themselves. The academic environment, it seems to me, sometimes fosters situations wherein scholars and teachers mistake our own sense of expansion in consciousness as that which should become our students'. In short, we lose the capacity to *listen* to our students.

I make this critique because I have recognized this tendency within my own practices. The demands of teaching Communicative Sexualities, however, have forced me to come to grips with this tendency in ways no other course has. I am a person with a particular sex life, a particular sexual history, and a particular gender orientation. I have particular ideas about what is "good sex" and "bad sex." I have deep-seated perspectives regarding sexual monogamy and partnership that are rooted in our shared U.S. American culture, and I am also someone who has had to fight consciously against the cultural norms which cultivated within me a sense of deviancy and badness for being a woman who experiences sexual desire for other women and not men. All of these factors, and more, are inescapably present to me in the classroom as I ask students to speak directly about their own sexual experience. There is simply no way I can create a safe, mature, and respectful space that is open to hearing very different perspectives and experiences of sexuality unless *I* can demonstrate an ability to speak about a wide variety of experiences from a wide variety of perspectives. Thus, I have had to develop a finely detailed understanding of my own preferences and perspectives because they will tend to dominate what I say and how I say it within the classroom. Equally important, I must be able to *hear* the particular and oftentimes subtle differences in the way students themselves talk about sexuality and their own sexual experiences. It is the *practice* of semiotic phenomenology that has allowed me to achieve a way of communicating with students in which these priorities can dominate. My successful teaching of the practice of semiotic phenomenology is possible only because of its conjunction with an advanced theoretical and philosophical study of it and the many intellectual traditions that help inform it.

My focus on the ethical and professional demands entailed in teaching Communicative Sexualities is necessary because I recognize just how easily sex can become a means of perpetuating human degradation, exploitation, and violence. In every classroom it is ultimately the teacher who is responsible for what happens within it. I think that issues related to sexuality are among the most consequential in our lives. Our public conflicts on issues related to sexuality only make the effort to recognize and cultivate healthy sexuality in our own lives more difficult. I very much believe that courses like Communicative Sexualities can benefit people of many ages, ranging from high school through advanced adulthood. I emphasize the demands of teaching such a course because it is all to common in our contemporary social environment for sex and sexuality to be reduced to titillations and a level of immaturity that prevent sexual expression from becoming a force for the development of healthy and fulfilling human relationships, and therefore healthy human communities as well.

The reader of this text will notice that I speak directly to college students. This text is, fundamentally, what I teach in Communicative Sexualities. I use many examples throughout this text, a large portion of which come directly from my experience teaching the course. Other examples are hypothetical, but all are informed by what I have learned over the years I have taught Communicative Sexualities. My effort in writing directly to college students has been to present the advanced theoretical and philosophical points in as plain an English as possible. I have referenced more advanced theoretical and philosophical works only as necessary. Yet, it would be a mistake to take this text to be exclusively, or even primarily, an undergraduate textbook. The focus on the *practical application* of semiotic phenomenology provides illustrations that will be very helpful for graduate students and researchers concerned with both qualitative methodology and gender studies/sexuality studies. The more advanced reader will find specific references to primary texts that will allow for more specialized study. I also include a list of suggested readings at the end of each chapter that will be of interest to those who wish to pursue further study.

Finally, I would like to speak directly to gay, lesbian, bisexual, transgendered, and transsexual students—basically, those who find themselves marked as sexual or gender "deviants" within our contemporary social world. My first impulse in developing and teaching Communicative Sexualities was to create a decidedly gay-friendly classroom environment in which we could speak freely and openly about our experiences and struggles. From my earliest experiences teaching at the college level, I have encountered innumerable students who have conveyed to me the many frustrations and fears associated with being in classrooms where they feel varying degrees of hostility and risk because of their sexual or gender orientation. Far too many young people today are tormented as they come to recognize themselves as gay, lesbian, bi, or trans. Far too many young people end up living in torment so severe that they come to consider taking their own lives. Far too many of them do. Far too often it is the case that this torment comes directly from peers at a time when peer groups have tremendous power to effect one's sense of self. Communicative Sexualities is part of my effort to cultivate ways of thinking and speaking about sexuality that promote healthy and fulfilling human relationships, especially for those who are confronted by social and interpersonal hostility.

Gay, lesbian, bi, and trans students often understand the reality of "heteronormativity" more sharply and acutely than heterosexual students. Over my years of teaching Communicative Sexualities, I have noticed a certain variability in each class's capacity to see and fully engage the reality of our "heteronormative" culture. The greater the variety of sexual orientations and experiences among the students in the class, and the greater our ability to bring those variations into our formal study, the more successful and insightful our research becomes. Straight students need non-straight students to see more of the reality of their experience, just as non-straight students need straight students to see more of the reality of their experience. A class made up of exclusively heterosexual students is just as limited as a class made up of exclusively nonheterosexual students. Each class will have its own difficulty in seeing beyond the heterosexual-homosexual binary.

The heterosexual-homosexual binary dominates our current understanding of sexuality and severely limits our capacity to see the realities of sexuality as experienced. It seems to me that heterosexuality will always be much more prominent within cultures than homosexuality, and this, in and of itself, is not necessarily bad. But, to take this binary to be a complete and accurate way of understanding sexuality prevents all of us from understanding what is actually at work within this binary distinction. In other words, it is important to recognize that we cannot simply do away with the hetero-homo binary—what matters is how we understand it and what we *do* with it. We must not ignore the vast array of convergences and divergences that are at work in this binary distinction—in short, we must see it with a {Both [Both/And] And [Either/Or]} logic. In working together and talking with each other we must be willing and able to see beyond the heterosexual-homosexual binary as a simple binary. Generally speaking, it is very difficult to do this in classes without gay, lesbian, bi, or trans students, or when classes with these students do not cultivate an environment where they can feel comfortable presenting those parts of themselves to their classmates.

Throughout my teaching career, I have sought to create classroom environments wherein human differences of all sorts are recognized and respected. This has also meant developing the ability to identify—and create alternate possibilities for—expressions of discomfort or disregard based on stereotypes or limited direct experience. This is a demanding task because in pursuing this goal it is easy to perpetuate overly simplified and presupposed value hierarchies that prevent the honest and direct examination of our thinking, feeling, and responding. The greater our ability to see and come to grips with the realities of our many human differences, the better able we will be to cultivate healthy human communities wherein the tendencies toward disrespect and disregard that can lead to degradation, exploitation, and violence will be lessened.

1

An Introduction to Sexuality as Subject Matter

Sexuality is personal, very personal. To think about it, to write about it, to feel it, or to act within it is to place some very personal part of oneself "out there" to be felt, experienced, seen, and responded to—even when we do so in complete privacy. This is because sexuality connects us to a world, a human world wherein even our most private intimate experience is infused with meaning and significance of which we are not the sole authors. Think about the ordinary and everyday way we move through our lives. As we pursue the normal activities of being in relationships with others—family and loved ones, friends, peers, colleagues, and acquaintances—we come to have experiences variously related to sexuality. We recognize our sexual desire for another. We are curious about our sexual desire and we talk with close friends. We think someone is interested in us sexually and we carefully try to assess the accuracy of our perception.

Sometimes we orchestrate these varying experiences. We recognize our desire and engage in activities that we hope will lead to a fulfillment of those desires. Other times they seem to emerge without our having anticipated them. We find ourselves in a situation where we become suddenly aware of an overt sexual expression toward us that we may or may not reciprocate. Sometimes those experiences seem to blend into the ongoing flow of our lives and fade into the background of what becomes our life history. Other times, our sexual experiences stand out among our other experiences and come to take a central place in how we come to understand ourselves and our lives well into our futures.

We do not decide how the social world in which we live will contextualize the meanings we come to make of our sexual experiences. We do not control the social or familial attitudes or practices through which we must travel in making our sexual experiences meaningful. Whatever sexuality is, and whatever it is to us, it becomes so by virtue of complex sets of relationships and practices that precede our existence and conscious awareness but of which we are also active participants. This is why we approach sexuality as a *communicative* phenomenon. To study sexuality as a communicative phenomenon means that we must learn to become very attentive to our experiences of sexuality, not just as something that we did or happened to us, but something that we both actively created and passively received.

Communicative sexualities as phenomena include a broad array of possible experiences. We can understand sexual desire as a physical desire that is different from a desire for companionship or friendship. On the other hand, these two desires can become one and the same. It can be the case, for example, that the desires for companionship and sexual fulfillment become mutually reinforcing. We see this when people who have been coupled for a long time describe each other as both lover and best friend. Other times, however, sexual fulfillment and the desire for companionship may be very much at odds. This is the case when people say things like, "we have great sex, but other than that we just don't seem to get along."

We can understand sexual desire as a phenomenon that is different from, say, the desire for respect from one's professional peers. But, if one works in a profession that is highly sexualized—like a movie star, or waitress whose uniform involves very little clothing—then these differences begin to blur. Even in professions that are not as highly sexualized, the question of sex appeal is often at issue in unspoken yet powerful ways. Women recognize this when they are critiqued in the workplace for dressing too provocatively, or not provocatively enough. A man working in an office where he is the only male may become very aware of and uncomfortable with the ways in which the women in his office examine and discuss his clothing and appearance.

To study communicative sexualities is to emphasize the pluralities of sexuality, which does not mean merely the plurality of sexual practices—although these are important, too. Rather, it means to study sexuality in the many ways that human beings come to perceive and express it. In this sense, sexuality can never be a singular phenomenon. To study communicative sexualities is to pursue an understanding of the complexities of sexual desire and fulfillment as we recognize and pursue them within the social and cultural contexts of our everyday lives. It means to become very attuned to the often conflicting and perplexing messages about sexuality that come from our family, peer groups, educational, religious, and political institutions, media, and so on, and how those messages contextualize our own experience and understanding.

To study communicative sexualities is to study sexuality as a private and intimate experience that is both of us and beyond us. This means that we must be willing to discover what we do not yet see. It means we must be able to question the fact of our seeing and understanding in order to more fully detail how it is that such a way of seeing and understanding became possible. In order to do this we must be able to examine the many presuppositions that inform our thinking about and experiencing of sexuality.

EXAMINING PRESUPPOSITIONS

When it comes to sexuality, there are many, many presuppositions that are in need of examination. Two are of particular importance: the heterosexual-homosexual distinction and our notions of what constitutes legitimate knowledge. Both of these presuppositions are deeply rooted in our own cultural sensibilities and are therefore difficult to set aside. It is often the case that even while we can fully understand and appreciate the scope and significance of these presuppositions, they remain tacitly at work in forming how we see and understand ourselves, others, and the world. To develop the capacity to see and interrogate the actual workings of our presuppositions in our perception is a difficult and demanding task. It is easy to deceive ourselves into thinking we have, for example, examined something from multiple perspectives, when in fact all we have done is alter our way of describing what we saw rather than actually see the same thing differently. One reason why it is so important that we become very adept at *seeing how* the presumption of heterosexuality is at work in our thinking and seeing, is because we will never be able to actually see heterosexuality if heterosexuality defines how we see sexuality.

When we talk about sexuality today, we often presume that we are talking about heterosexuality and homosexuality as a fundamental and accurate classification. This classification is not symmetrical, however, because it carries the presumption that heterosexuality is natural and homosexuality is not. This distinction does not function neutrally, but rather as a strongly enforced division whereby nonheterosexuals are "marked" and often held in suspicion. The heterosexual-homosexual distinction is clearly central in many ways to much of what we understand and experience when it comes to sexuality. One does not have to "come out" as a heterosexual, and however confounding sexual self-discovery is for heterosexuals, such discovery remains largely within an implicitly understood and accepted norm. The fact is that if one recognizes a same-sex sexual desire within himself or herself, that recognition creates problems of self-discovery that are often far more complex and dangerous than the sexual self-discovery pursued by heterosexuals. The complexity and danger in this process is largely a result of how our cultural sensibilities of what is good or moral is aligned with the heterosexual-homosexual distinction.

It is also true that however powerful the heterosexual-homosexual distinction is as a culturally-based norm infused with a clear value hierarchy, it is the case that this distinction alone tells us very little about the actual experiences people have in the processes of sexual self-discovery. It would be a mistake to presume simply that for heterosexuals sexual self-discovery occurs without internal conflict, while for homosexuals conflict defines sexual self-discovery. There are certainly ways in which this is true, but we will only distort the reality of our experience if we retain this basic presumption as an essential truth of our cultural sensibilities about sexuality today. What we each personally "know" about sexuality, especially as we experience it in our everyday lives, is far more complex and intricate than anything captured in something so general and indistinct as the heterosexual-homosexual labels. It is also important to note that our notions of "sexual morality" are particularly impoverished to the degree that they rely on this highly limited distinction.

The second presupposition, concerning our notions of what constitutes legitimate knowledge, is also deeply bound within our culturally rooted taken-for-granted ways of seeing and understanding. Like the heterosexual-homosexual distinction, our basic notions of what constitutes legitimate knowledge are often difficult to see and understand because they remain tacitly at work in forming how we see and understand ourselves, others, and the world. Our own cultural dispositions place a high value on rationality and rational thought. We believe deeply in the idea that we can think through the problems and predicaments of the day and arrive at the best understanding of things through rational thought. Because of this deeply held belief—which we will *not* abandon in our study of sexualities—it is easy for us to believe that we have exhausted the possibilities for seeing and understanding without ever having touched, much less detailed, our deeply seated and habitual patterns of perception.

Culturally, we hold deep belief in the possibilities of "pure" science—that is, science untouched by the fact and variability of human perception and expression. We tend to believe deeply that the world can become known as it exists separately from the particularity of any one person's perception or experience. These beliefs are embodied in the social science approach to the study of human beings. The social sciences do, indeed, provide us with important information that contributes to our understanding of things. In and of themselves, however, the social sciences tend to forget that they are able to provide that important information precisely and solely because human beings bring the fact of their own experience and understanding into the information generated via social science approaches.

For our part, we will not forget the fact that anything that becomes significant to human beings does so because of the fact of human participation in it. This means that we cannot leave out the fact of our own human participation in our study. We cannot do this because the significance and meaningfulness of the things we study *precede our study of them*. To pretend that we study anything in a vacuum, outside of own sense of what is significant and meaningful, is to deny the most important fact of how we come to experience and understand ourselves, others, and the world.

Thus, to take up a formal study of our sexual experience and the meaningfulness we come to make of that experience requires an approach different from our commonly recognized notion of social science research. The social sciences are, for the most part, presumed to be neutral and objective in their study of human beings and the social world. Neutrality and objectivity are explicit goals of social science research. This social science perspective seems quite natural and correct to us because many of the presumptions that inform the social science approach to knowledge resonate deeply within our own U.S. American culture sensibilities. We often presume that social science research provides the most objective, accurate account and understanding of things possible.

Such an approach is inadequate for studying sexuality as it is experienced and made meaningful in our lives because the complexities and intricacies of those experiences are prefigured and often concealed in the effort to name, label, define, categorize, or organize "sexuality" as a discrete body of knowledge. Before we even get a chance to examine the fact of our sexual experience, we are strapped with sets of terms and concepts that have already codified how we should understand it.

Rather than a social science approach to our study of sexuality, we will be taking a *human science* approach grounded in *Communicology* (Lanigan, 1972, 1977, 1984, 1988, 1992). The major difference between the social sciences and the human sciences is the degree to which each problematizes the fact of human perception in our ability to ascertain what is a real and accurate account of human beings and our social world. The social sciences tend to problematize the fact of human perception only marginally in that human perception is recognized to be variable and inconsistent. The problem, from a social science point of view, is one of making human perception as precise and consistent as possible through methodological commitments which hold that the world exterior to human consciousness and experience exists in a way that is predictable and knowable outside of any particular human being's perception.

The human sciences, in contrast, problematize the fact of human perception as a central feature of any and all efforts to ascertain what is a real and accurate account of human beings and their social world. This means that human scientists feature the fact and presence of human consciousness and experience as irreducibly present and active in all human perception. Human perception and the fact of human consciousness and experience must therefore be accounted for in our effort to ascertain what might be real beyond any particular perception or understanding. Our effort to account for human perception and the fact of human consciousness and experience will be taken up largely through the examples I provide throughout the text. As we go through these examples that are designed to focus our thinking on these problems as they are related to sexuality, it is important to keep in mind that the problem of human consciousness and experience has occupied some of the greatest thinkers of human history, and has led to the production of a vast array of scholarship tracing through the entire history of Western thought. Our concerns, however, will follow Lanigan and address the work of Edmund Husserl, Charles Sanders Peirce, Roman Jakobson, and Maurice Merleau-Ponty.

Communicology is "the study of human discourse in all its embodied forms ranging from speech and language to gesture and signs." Communicology "uses the methodology of *semiotic phenomenology* in which the expressive body discloses cultural codes, and cultural codes shape the perceptive body—an ongoing, dialectical, complex helix of twists and turns constituting the reflectivity, reversibility, and reflexivity of consciousness and experience" (Lanigan, 2008, p. 855). As we move through our study of our experience of sexuality we will continue to develop this notion of the interrelationships between the expressive body as it discloses cultural codes, and cultural codes as they shape the perceptive body. Because we are interested in a direct and thoroughgoing examination of sexuality as we experience it, we will apply semiotic phenomenology as a research methodology in our examination of these complex interrelationships. That means that we will need to spend a great deal of time thinking about our own experience in terms of how our bodies express our cultural codes, and how our cultural codes shape our body's capacity to perceive. Our communicological approach and use of semiotic phenomenology will allow us to continue to examine the two presuppositions just detailed, as well the many others we will come to see as we pursue our study.

A TOUCHY AND HIGH-STAKES SUBJECT

Consider the fact that sexuality itself—that is, the fact that our lived-experiences of sexuality—can be as joyfully and passionately shared as they can be humanly degrading and isolating. Moreover, the degree to which we experience sexuality as one extreme or the other often has nothing to do with the specific sexual acts performed. What one person finds degrading another can find fulfilling. It is also true that over the span of one's life, something which one experienced as sexually distasteful becomes enjoyable later in life. There is simply no doubt that the phenomenon of "sexuality" as it is lived, pursued, experienced, and made meaningful by human beings traverses a terrain of possibilities which far exceed any effort to define or know it as a singular or static thing.

I focus on this point because, as we shall see, this deep-seated tendency, rooted in our U.S. American cultural sensibilities, to think that we can "know" and understand sexuality separately from our personal experience of it predominates in ways we are almost always unaware of. Such a way of thinking means that we often feel satisfied in our understanding of what we think sexuality is or should be without consciously (much less, seriously) considering the fact of our own experience. In this circumstance it is possible for people to understand their own feelings of sexual violation as unproblematic. We must not be satisfied with our taken-for-granted presumptions about what sexuality is or should be. We must, in every case, be committed to an open and thoroughgoing search for the complexities of our thinking and feeling as they are related to the immediacy of our lived-experiences of sexuality.

The very fact that our experience of sexuality cannot be so easily defined means that our study of it cannot be governed by the unexamined judgments commonly circulating in our public (especially political) discourse. It is a risky endeavor to present and study sexuality as we experience it. It is difficult enough to talk about one's sexual experience with one's intimate partner, much less in a college classroom with classmates and peers who are, in all likelihood, mostly strangers. And, on top of that, I am asking that we do this at a time when the politics of issues related to sexuality are at as fevered a temperature as ever. The incidence of sexual crimes within our society never seems to abate, and even some of our most trusted spiritual leaders and outspoken political advocates of sexual morality have been exposed as sexual criminals.

It is precisely for all of these reasons that we must begin addressing the fact of our sexual experience directly, honestly, and in a thoroughgoing way. The stakes are very high, not just because sexuality is such a volatile public issue, but more because how we experience ourselves sexually often has a tremendous impact on our most deeply felt sense of self. Late adolescence and early adulthood are the times in life when we expect people to begin developing a sexual self-awareness, and learning about their sexual desires and how to pursue fulfillment of those desires with others. We might call these the "formative years" of what will become our mature, adult sexual relationships. How we learn to think and feel about sexuality during these "formative years" can have a powerful and long-lasting effect on our lives.

The stakes are high for yet another reason. If we are lucky, our late adolescence and early adulthood do indeed provide us with the kind of learning opportunities whereby, through the sometimes difficult and confusing process of trial and error, we come to develop a sexual self-awareness that is fulfilling in ways that cultivate a healthy sense of ourselves and our intimate sexual partners. But not everyone is so lucky, and we must recognize the fact that, for many people, the development of sexual self-awareness has nothing to do with exploring one's own interests and desires. It is far too often the case that our sexual self-awareness is forced upon us through the violence and manipulations of sexual assault, molestation, and incest. To learn about sexuality in this way damages us, to put it mildly.

Forced or imposed silence about sexual violation is one of the ways through which its negative effects are sustained within us, our families, and our communities. I think it is difficult for the average college student who has not experienced sexual violation of any sort to really grasp just how high the stakes are for people who have been victims of sexual violence when they begin to look directly at their experience of sexual violence and the meanings they and others ascribe to it. At the same time, however, survivors of sexual violence often, over time and with a adequate support from family and loved ones, come to a much deeper awareness of their own sexuality and a much greater sensitivity to the circumstances in their own lives that cultivate a positive and thriving life. We have much to gain by attending carefully to our own and others' experiences of sexuality.

Attending to our own and others' sexual experiences requires a great deal of maturity and respect for human difference. This is crucially important because if one pursues the kind of direct and open study that I am suggesting without a high level of maturity and respect, then it is very possible that our effort to study sexuality can in fact become a mechanism of subtle, but very real, sexual violence. Our judgment about what is good or bad about sexuality must be suspended while we take a direct and thoroughgoing examination of our lived-experiences of it. It is crucially important that in looking directly at our lived-experience of sexuality, we develop the ability to become highly attuned to the many prejudgments that contextualize the meanings we come to ascribe to our own and others' sexual experience. We must be very careful to recognize when our thinking is governed by taken-for-granted presumptions about what sexuality is or should be.

There is no a priori guide which can guarantee that sexual expression, or our study of it, will elevate toward a deeply human achievement of connection, or degrade toward a profoundly dehumanizing experience. To study our lived-experience of sexuality therefore requires a keen awareness of this dual potential of sexuality. That means that we must understand the potential for sexuality to be experienced positively as a great expanse of human intimacy and connection, but we must not succumb to the tendency to idealize sexuality in this way. Rather, it is important that we recognize this greatly positive human connection that can be cultivated through our shared sexual experiences because it stands in sharp and true distinction from expressions of sexuality that are experienced as degrading and dehumanizing. We keep the idea of sexuality as one kind of expression through which our highest ideals of human intimacy and connection can be established so that we can take a very sober and direct look at exactly what we experience.

Ideals are ideals because they are rarely fully achieved, and never absolutely sustainable. Ideals are striven for, but the totality of our personal or shared experience is never fully encapsulated by them. In order to guard against the easy idealization of sexuality as an exemplar of our most humanly affirming experiences we must be willing to suspend our presuppositions about what sexuality is or should be and look directly at sexuality as we experience it. Consider again how it is possible, perhaps even common, for people to have a sexual experience that is degrading, yet chalk it up to just the way things happen sometimes (or, all the time). If we fail to examine how it is that this particular sexual experience felt degrading, then it becomes highly likely that we will allow ourselves to have similar experiences in the future. Sometimes, we hold our idealizations of sexuality so strongly that we cannot see the reality of our actual experience. This happens when we say to ourselves, "but he [or she] really does love me." The notion of love, as pure idea and/or idealization, can be so powerful as to override the reality of a relationship characterized by violence.

It is a difficult thing to understand so clearly what our cultural and social world expects from "love" as it should be experienced in sexual activity, and then ask oneself if one's experience really is "love." It is very clear to me, after nearly a decade of working with college students on this topic, that their desire and need to maintain the sense that their own sexual experience fulfills this ideal of "love" so commonly dominates their thinking that they have a very difficult time looking directly at the immediate and concrete experience of sexuality as they lived it. I believe that this phenomenon of taking refuge in an ideal is motivated in large part by the many understandable fears that arise from addressing the kinds of questions I am asking students to address.

In order to counter this tendency toward idealization it is important that we focus on the immediacy of our lived-experiences of sexuality. This means talking about our physical body, what it does and how it feels. This means much more than simply being able to use biological terms like "penis," "clitoris," "vagina," "anus," "breasts," "nipples," "tongue," and so on. It means being able to think and speak in direct and blunt terms about what our bodies do—bodies get hot and moist; nipples, penises, and clitorises get swollen and hard; we use our bodies to feel, caress, suck, press, enter into each other. Sometimes we "make love," but other times we are just "fucking." Sometimes our bodies experience sexual activity as fulfilling a need for an intensely shared intimacy with a very particular person, and sometimes our bodies experience sexual activity as responding to a voracious hunger that simply needs to be satiated.

Perhaps the reader finds the preceding paragraph a little shocking, or "inappropriate." It is certainly a "dangerous" paragraph to write for many reasons, but two are important to mention. First, there is the reality of the political context in which we live, and it occurs to me that these words are ripe for censorship for simply appearing on a written page of a book meant to be used in a college classroom (I live and work in the state of Arizona, whose legislature has a history of scrutinizing our university curriculum and calling for syllabi to include "opt out" clauses for any material students might find potentially offensive; the legislature also has a history of calling for the elimination of "women's studies"). But secondly, and more importantly, using the language as I use it above can easily degrade our thinking into a "titillating" orientation that encourages an immaturity that is absolutely contrary to the substance and process required for the successful study of our lived-experience of sexuality. The language I use in the preceding paragraph is accurate, and this is why, for better or worse, it makes such an impact. The language itself reveals the fact that the very same sexual acts are equally capable of being experienced as humanly affirming or humanly degrading. It is precisely because this language carries the possibility of degrading our thinking into a "titillating" or immature orientation that we must use it. Only by fully recognizing the ways in which our thinking about and studying sexuality can degrade into a dehumanizing orientation may we be able to come to adequately distinguish between a "good" and "bad" sexuality.

COMMUNICATIVE SEXUALITIES

Today we commonly understand sexuality as a property of persons, as an aspect of our internal self that is reflected in our thinking and feeling, and is observable to others in the way we behave—in short, as an identity. We understand sexuality as a drive or desire, as something rooted within us that directs us toward specific people, to seek out specific kinds of relationships, and pursue certain kinds of interactions. We often presume sexuality to be something we have within us that seeks expression and fulfillment. And we all recognize that as we seek expression and fulfillment, we must navigate our sexual expressions through complex sets of social values, group relationships, interpersonal relationships, and private contemplations. At some points we may feel satisfied and fulfilled, at other points frustrated and unfulfilled. We may feel certain about the difference between fulfilled and unfulfilled sexual expression, or we may feel quite confused about what exactly makes the difference. Often, how we feel about our sexual interactions bears a strong influence about how we feel about ourselves as persons.

The point here is to consider that when we presume that sexuality is "ours," that it is a property or aspect of ourselves for which we seek expression with other people, we miss what is, in fact, the most significant aspect of sexuality itself—that whatever sexuality is to us, it becomes so through our *communicative practices.* To study "communicative sexualities" is to take up the study of sexuality *not* as a property of persons, like what we typically think of as a "personality characteristic." To do that is to presume that sexuality exists internally within each of us, and this puts us in the position of having to figure out how we want to express that internal sexuality externally, in the world of other people. This way of understanding sexuality, as a property of persons, keeps us away from the very way in which sexuality comes to be what it is for each of us. To study "communicative sexualities" is to locate the phenomenon of sexuality within the intricacies of our immediate and embodied interconnection with the social and cultural world in which we are situated. The discipline of communicology, and its methodological expression as semiotic phenomenology, allows us to do just that.

How we come to understand "sexuality," whatever that may be within our own private experiencing, is a manifestation of the fact that human beings exist within social groups that are fundamentally interconnected by virtue of shared space, common history, common language, and common cultural practices. Not all persons living in the same space at the same time will come to privately experience sexuality in the same way, but our fundamental interconnectedness means that our own private experiencing is never independent or merely idiosyncratic. This common interconnectedness is sustained in the fact that we shared space, histories, languages, and cultural practice means that whatever our particular experience of sexuality, it is actualized only by virtue of the communicative processes in which we are always and inescapably *situated.*

Our study of sexuality, therefore, must feature these complex interconnections in which we are situated. It is from our location within the specific times and places of our life experiences that we come to have the particular understanding and awareness of sexuality that we do. Although, this is *not* to say that we can reduce our understanding and awareness of sexuality to the facts entailed in our location, or situatedness in a social, historical, and cultural world. We must develop a two-part sensitivity that includes both the shared codes of our time, place, and practices; and our lived-experience as it becomes manifest to us in the immediacy of our everyday lives. Our study of communicative sexualities begins with the fact of lived-experience, *not* because our own individual experience constitutes some essential truth about ourselves or sexuality, but simply because *our lived-experience of it is the only direct access we have to it.*

Whatever we really know about sexuality, we know because we embody it. Our ability to attend to this knowing about sexuality in our embodiment of it is what this text seeks to cultivate. As we begin our study of communicative sexualities, we must cultivate the conceptual and practical ability to *see ourselves seeing* in the particular ways that we do. We need to begin to see the presuppositions at work in the ways we think about and experience sexuality, and learn to suspend those so that we may consider their adequacy for understanding sexuality as we live it and experience it in the context of a shared world.

PROCEEDING FORWARD

In this introductory chapter I have sketched my overall approach to the study of our lived-experience of sexuality. I have emphasized the serious and demanding nature of such a study, and argued that a social science perspective is inadequate for a serious study of sexuality as it is lived, experienced, and made meaningful in the concrete immediacy of our everyday lives. Communicology provides the logic and process through which we can systematically examine the ways in which our "expressive body discloses cultural codes, and cultural codes shape the perceptive body" (Lanigan, 2008, p. 855). I have explained why it is crucial from the start that we be willing—and able to learn how—to suspend our presuppositions about sexuality so that we may focus on its reality as experienced.

As we move forward from here, we will take up the practical task of learning about and examining our presuppositions concerning sexuality. In chapter 2, Our Lived-Experience of Sexuality as the Subject of Research, I focus specifically on what we need to do in order to turn our attention to our lived-experience of sexuality. In the first part of the chapter, I provide descriptions of the challenges at work in pursuing a direct and thoroughgoing examination of our lived-experience of sexuality. I emphasize the importance of creating a mature and safe classroom environment, and illustrate some of the ways in which such an environment can be cultivated. In the second part of the chapter, I begin the process of "clearing the conceptual space" through which we will come to examine our lived-experience of sexuality. The point here is to take as full account as initially possible of our basic presuppositions regarding sexuality as a biological, social, and cultural phenomenon. Throughout this section of the chapter I pose questions directly to readers that are designed to reveal how these basic presuppositions have been at work in their own life experience. At this beginning stage of our study, it is important to take account of as many of the taken-for-granted terms and conditions through which we come to our experience as possible. I conclude this chapter with a consideration of sexual practices and the problem of sexual violence.

Whereas chapter 2 prompts serious examination of our taken-for-granted presumptions about sexuality as we have learned them personally, chapter 3, History, Time, Context, prompts an examination of the cultural aspects of sexuality as a shared historical and temporal phenomenon. My purpose in this chapter is to illustrate the importance of historicity and temporality as they are present in lived-experience. This chapter asks readers to reflect on the fact and circumstance of the social, historical, and cultural contexts in which they have come to have the particular experiences of their own lives. There is no doubt that young people today think differently from those of my generation with regard to gender expectations and sexual self-determination. At the same time, however, to presume that we have "moved beyond" previous generations instantly stalls any effort to ascertain exactly what that "moving beyond" does and does not entail. I pay particular attention to the inevitable gap between what we believe ourselves to believe, and what we actually believe as revealed in the immediacy of our experience and behavior. As in chapter 2, I pose questions directly to readers that are designed to reveal how the historical context of their own lives has been at work in the way they have come to understand themselves, others, and the world. The effort in this chapter is to raise specific questions concerning the historical context at work for readers in their everyday lives at the present time.

Having taken up the effort to consider the many presuppositions we have come to have about sexuality in the specific social, historical, and cultural circumstances of our time, we shift to a discussion of the theoretical and philosophical terms through which we pursue our communicological study. Chapter 4, Semiotics in Communicology, establishes some of the basic theoretical concepts that inform communicology. These theoretical concepts are introductory and feature key aspects of communication through which we can begin to detail the complex interrelationship between our conscious awareness and our shared cultural habits or patterns of communicating. Careful examination of this interrelationship helps reveal the very points at which it became possible for our experience to have become what it did. I make specific reference to structuralism, and highlight the difference between what I refer to as a rigidly structuralist approach and the phenomenological structuralism presented in the work of Roman Jakobson (1990). These are key points taken up by Lanigan in the development of communicology and its methodology of semiotic phenomenology. The focus on diachrony and synchrony, apperception and context, the paradigmatic and syntagmatic axes of language, and marked and unmarked terms aims to provide students with some basic concepts that can assist in examining what is present in the immediacy of our sense-making.

In chapter 5, Phenomenology in Communicology, I argue that because human existence is inescapably intersubjective, our typical sense of ourselves as in possession of an "identity" is fundamentally flawed. Whatever our sense of ourselves is, it is an ongoing achievement that is *contingent*. Communication is the basic and most important constituent of this contingency. It is through the contingencies of communication that our intersubjective existence enables the dynamic and ongoing achievement that we come to recognize as *experience*.

In order to illustrate these contingencies of communication, I detail the four primary networks of communication as presented by Ruesch and Bateson (1951, 1987). I offer an extended example to show how these four networks are present in the immediacy of lived-experience. The point here is to illustrate the particular value of directing phenomenological attention to communication. Seeing communication from a phenomenological perspective requires an understanding of the difference between communication theory and information theory. A discussion of this very important point concludes the chapter.

The discussion of semiotics and phenomenology in communicology paves the way for the presentation of the methodology of semiotic phenomenology. Chapter 6, Semiotic Phenomenology, provides a detailed discussion of semiotic phenomenology as an applied research procedure. Thus the discussion of semiotic phenomenology features those aspects that most directly inform its application. The significance of human speech as an essential point in the convergence between person and culture is considered. This convergence highlights the need for a methodology that is both recursive and synergistic. A discussion of the relationship between semiotic phenomenological theory and semiotic phenomenological methodology demonstrates how these recursive and synergistic aspects inform the research practice. The basic research steps of phenomenological description, phenomenological reduction, and phenomenological interpretation are detailed, and specific terminology of phenomenology is introduced. The crucial distinction between the "order of analysis" and the "order of experience" as it functions in applied research is discussed. Following this discussion, a brief or "shorthand" version of the procedures of semiotic phenomenology is offered.

Chapter 7, Semiotic Phenomenology Applied, addresses the specific process of selecting a topic for and then conducting semiotic phenomenological research. The examination of presuppositions and the invocation of the phenomenological epoché are illustrated through a discussion of research conducted by students in my Communicative Sexualities course. The process of identifying phenomena related to sexual experience that are conducive to phenomenological research is discussed, and the three steps of phenomenological research—description, reduction, and interpretation—are illustrated.

Chapter 8, Cultural Ethics and Personal Obligations, considers the issues at stake when we begin to assess the reality of sexuality as it is lived and experienced by persons. It considers the crucial connection between persons, personal experience, and the communities in which people live, and the many challenges facing teachers and students in a course such as Communicative Sexualities. This chapter address the question as to how we might go about differentiating "bad" from "good" expressions of sexuality, and considers this in the context of communities wherein generational cycles of sexual and relational violence are common.

FOR FURTHER READING

Ernst Cassir, *The Logic of the Cultural Sciences* (New Haven, Conn.: Yale University Press, 2000).

Eve Kosofsky Sedgwick, "Introduction: Axiomatic," in *Epistemology of the Closet* (Berkeley: University of California Press, 1990), 1–63.

Lester Embree, "Human Sciences," in *Encyclopedia of Phenomenology*, ed. Lester Embree et al. (Boston: Kluwer Academic Publishers, 1997), 315–20.

2

Our Lived-Experience of Sexuality as the Subject of Research

As we begin the process of learning how to study sexuality in the immediacy of our lived-experience, it is important that we develop a shared conceptual understanding of the subject matter at hand. We must use this shared conceptual understanding as a basis for a study that can move us beyond the limits and presumptions inherent in this very conceptual apparatus itself. Developing this shared conceptual understanding makes it easier to talk about our lived-experiences of sexuality because we can recognize the commonalities of our experiences within this conceptual apparatus and thus feel less concern about how others will perceive us.

To study any kind of lived-experience, but especially our lived-experience of sexuality, requires a very different way of thinking than what guides us as we move through the activities of our everyday lives. We need to learn how to become keenly aware of *how* we are thinking, of *how* the most basic conceptualizations of what is real for us are at work in our thinking, and *how* our own personal experiences intersect with our social and cultural upbringing to lead us to think and see in the ways that we do. As we move into the more advanced stages of our study, we will find that even this initial attention to how we are thinking and experiencing itself requires an ongoing examination. It is never enough to have taken a single effort at seeing how we see, think, feel, and experience. Our movement through our research study will give us the opportunity to understand the fact of our experiencing in more and more intricate terms.

Making our thinking itself an object of our thinking has a very distinct benefit when it comes to studying our experience of sexuality: It allows us to step outside of what we experienced and thought a moment ago and make it an "object" of our observation. As a result, the common, powerful, and often unconscious attachments we have to our way of thinking about ourselves as sexual beings can be loosened, and we feel less threatened by the idea of exploring how sexuality is meaningful to us in our lives. It then becomes much easier to share our thinking and feeling with others. As a result it becomes possible to engage in a process of systematically examining what in fact has made it possible for us to come to have experienced sexuality in the way that we did. It removes some of the personal investment we have in the "correctness," "accuracy," or "normalness" of our thinking, seeing, and feeling; and thereby makes it easier to look at and talk about what we have in fact experienced in the immediacy of being sexual.

TALKING ABOUT SEX IN THE COLLEGE CLASSROOM

Imagine, if you will, walking into a college classroom on the first day of class and being told that the entire sixteen-week semester is going to focus on a direct examination of our own sexual experiences. This is the position some two hundred or so students have faced when they have walked into my classroom over the many years that I have taught this course. You can imagine the tension in the room. At some point in each of the classes I have taught, sometimes very early in the semester and sometimes not until later, students come to speak in a way that moves beyond these tensions and allows us to understand that once we assume the stance of genuine respect toward ourselves and our experience it becomes possible to explore the reality of what we actually experience. When this happens, the classroom becomes a space where we can directly and honestly explore our experience of sexuality without the fear of criticism or judgment, especially self-judgment. And, it has been my experience in teaching this subject matter, that the judgments we make about ourselves often have far more destructive power than the judgments others make of us—although, those are very real and can be very destructive as well.

My most stark experience of a student speaking up in a class in a way that establishes a heightened sense of respect for himself and his classmates occurred within the first two weeks of one particular course. I almost always generate discussion early in the semester by asking students to talk about what happened when they had the "birds and bees" discussion with their parents or some other adult in their lives. I expand the question by asking how it is they first learned about sex, not from movies or television, but from people in their lives who they look up to for guidance. In this particular class, the students began by conveying some of the more typical responses. One young man says, "My dad sat me down, handed me some condoms and said, 'Son, be smart.'" A young woman says, "Well, really it was my peer group more than anything else. My parents never really said anything except that they argued about when I could start dating." And then a young man spoke up and said, "I learned about sex when I was ten years old and my uncle molested me."

Dead silence took hold in the classroom. I was shocked since I never expected a student to make such a disclosure so early and assertively in the class. The student was clearly not distressed in the way he spoke those words, and by the tonality and nonverbal aspects of his speech you'd think he was talking about going out for dinner last night. I paused for a moment while I got my bearings and we all took in the gravity of what he said. Then I responded as if this were a completely normal thing for some-one to say because I know that in every class I teach it is highly likely that there is at least one student whose introduction to sexuality was forced upon them in one way or another. I responded to the student by saying something to the effect of, "Thank you for being brave enough to share that with us. Unfortunately, you are not alone in coming to learn about sexuality in this way. Many, many people have very similar experiences." I probably went on about the prevalence of sexual violence in our society and the importance of recognizing that. We continued on with the dis-cussion and other students returned to offering their more benign experi-ences of talking with older brothers and sisters, and so on. In relatively quick order, this particular classroom of students elevated their level of maturity, respect, and honesty to levels that have surpassed any other class I have taught—and every class I have taught on this subject rises to a high level of maturity and mutual respect.

The point I am trying to get at here is *not* that students should be willing and able to disclose their most private intimate experience with a group full of strangers within the first few weeks of a new semester. No, no, no, not at all. The point I am getting at is that this extraordinary student, who by all outward appearances was very masculine, attractive, physically fit, an all-American kind of guy, who I might otherwise have stereotyped as a "frat boy," had himself worked through the many challenges of becoming a survivor of homosexual incest and emerging with a profoundly strong sense of self-understanding and self-respect.

What made the difference for this particular class was that this student's disclosure established that even the most taboo sexual experience, which exacts some of the most psychologically damaging effects upon a child, can come to be understood without the shame, self-blame, and disintegrating self-respect that so often come with incest and other kinds of sexual vio-lence. This student's disclosure revealed to us, in ways that I think none of us could fully comprehend at the moment, that our own sense of human dignity and self-respect can be so powerful as to make pale by comparison the more easily discussed topics like having sex with someone despite not really wanting to. The initial fears we might have had about sharing our own experience were greatly lessened because we had all experienced the power of this student's own dignity and self-respect.

This student's disclosure also revealed immediately to us just how much ground there is to travel within ourselves to fully grasp the significance of understanding ourselves as sexual beings. His disclosure revealed that the more directly and honestly we can travel across this high-stakes terrain of self-understanding, the more contact we can come to have with our own sense of human dignity and the more strongly we can cultivate and sustain genuine respect for ourselves and others. This student's disclosure had a profoundly positive impact on the class that was sustained throughout the entire sixteen weeks of the course.

Creating a Mature, Respectful, and Safe Classroom

At this point, I want us to pause and shift our thinking. This extraordinary young man's disclosure is the exception, not the rule. I have discussed it at some length because it illustrates the high stakes and high demands at work in a college classroom where the primary objective is a direct and thoroughgoing study of our lived-experience of sexuality. But, his disclosure also made it much easier than usual for me to fulfill my responsibilities as the teacher to create a mature, safe, and fundamentally respectful classroom environment. That is, this young man's disclosure and presence in the classroom achieved pretty much instantly the kind of mature, safe, and fundamentally respectful classroom atmosphere that I must work diligently to cultivate from the first moment of the class through to its very end. This extraordinary student made it easy for me to cultivate a classroom environment in which a very serious, safe, open, and deeply respectful process of reflecting on our sexual experience could emerge.

It is important in our study of our lived-experience of sexuality that we consider carefully what is required to cultivate this kind of serious and safe classroom environment without the aid of such a profoundly personal self-disclosure as that offered by the student described above. I never, under any circumstances, expect or require students to disclose anything about their personal experience that they are not comfortable disclosing. I make this point as explicitly as I can in the first meeting of the class, and I emphasize it throughout the first third of the class at least. Because I allow students to move slowly into the idea of talking explicitly about their sexual experience, it is important that we begin the class by establishing a shared and recognized sense of respect and humility related to our self-understanding. One way of achieving this is to acknowledge that we all have *presuppositions* about ourselves, others, and our social world. An examination of these presuppositions helps us understand the things we have in common. The first and most important presupposition we must examine is the notion that we already know the full scope and impact of our sexual experience and the meaningfulness it holds in our self-understanding.

As human beings we can never be fully transparent to ourselves. We can never really know ourselves fully. It is hard to imagine that any human being could ever fully comprehend all of the things present and at work in the immediacy of lived-experience. We are too interconnected with all the complexities of our cultural norms, social environment, and personal histories to be able to sort through things and somehow see the totality of who we are. Moreover, once we begin to reflect on who we are, that act in and of itself alters how we will come to experience ourselves in the future. Self-understanding and self-knowledge are not static. Rather, they are an ongoing achievement that we can cultivate through self-reflection. Self-reflection allows us to look back over our experience and come to see things that were present in our experience but of which we were unaware.

Let's say, for example, that I had a misunderstanding with my very good and trusted friend who later tells me that I am not a good listener. Since I pride myself on being a good listener, I am at first offended that my friend could say such a thing. My gut-level reaction is that my friend is wrong. But because I trust my friend I have second thoughts and wonder if my friend might be right. I begin reflecting back on my experience and wonder if my perception about yesterday's misunderstanding is accurate. And, when I come to our next conversation, the idea that my friend thinks I am not a good listener remains in the back of my mind, and because of that I am "in" that conversation differently than I would have been otherwise. I am more self-aware of how I am listening. But still, it is difficult to say that I "know" how good a listener I am or am not. All I can know is that I am more conscious of how I am listening. As I am paying more attention to how I am listening, I may come to find *evidence* that I am in fact listening better, because what was an impasse in my understanding of my friend's perspective yesterday is no longer so today.

Thus it is true that *act of reflecting* in the present on how we have experienced and understood ourselves in the past, alters how we will experience and understand ourselves in the future. Yet, what we come to reflect on is never only a matter of our personal free choice. What we actually come to reflect on about ourselves is influenced by both our own sense of self and the many influences of the world outside our self. The ongoing development of our self-awareness and self-understanding is *both constrained and enabled* by the semiotics—signs, codes, and meanings—of everyday interaction as they are provided to us by our cultural, social, and familial worlds. If being a "good listener" were not a cultural or social value that we took to be personally relevant to our self-understanding, then our friend's comment would be irrelevant to us, and we would not alter our way of reflecting on or attending to how we listen.

Now, consider the difference between reflecting on being a "good listener" or not, as compared to being a "good sex partner" or not, or being "sexually molested" or not. Each idea impacts us personally, but the stakes seem much higher when we shift from thinking about how others perceive our listening ability to our sexual "ability," and even higher when we shift our thinking to having been sexual violated. How we reflect on ourselves as sexual beings is very much connected to the meanings of sex and sexuality as provided for us by our cultural and social world.

In order to begin the process of learning how to study our lived-experience of sexuality, we must examine the cultural codes and social meanings through which we come to understand ourselves as sexual beings. These are the codes and meanings made available to us independently of our experience. We cannot make our experience meaningful except through those terms and sensibilities provided by our social and cultural world, but those terms and sensibilities cannot fully dictate or determine how we will make our experience meaningful. Consider, for example, what happens when those cultural codes and social meanings cultivate a sense of shame for simply having sexual desire (i.e., a woman who is lustful is a whore). At the very least, it makes it difficult to come to a sense of self-respect for oneself as a sexual being.

Thus it is that when we come together with others seeking sexual intimacy, we do so within contexts that include varying degrees of awareness of ourselves, others, and the social meanings and cultural codes at work. We all have complex life histories and desires that set the ground upon which we must travel in making our experience meaningful. To recognize, for example, that one's sexual desire is directed toward members of the same sex is, within our heteronormative social world, to also immediately know, without having to reflect on it, that one should be very careful about expressing that desire. This is why such a thing as "the closet" can exist. We all have to navigate through the social and cultural pressures brought by the communities in which we live. The more "outside" of the norm we are—and there are many ways "straight" people can be "outside" of the norm—the more consequential are the particulars of how we navigate through them. The complexities of these circumstances mean that no matter how clear and firm we are in our own sense of sexual selves or in our sexual ideals, the actual pursuit and achievement of those ideals is rarely straightforward.

I want a long-term committed relationship based in trust and mutual respect. I want a life-partner with whom I share passions, interests and a common understanding of what it means to live a "good life." I can be very clear on this desire. So can the person I am in a relationship with. But, as we all know, even though clarity about these ideals helps, they are a very far way from achieving them in our actual lives. Thus, whether we are talking about ideals of partnership, ideals of romance and love, ideals of physical pleasure, ideals of sexual mastery or seduction, or ideals of sexual freedom and the like, in all cases those ideals must be recognized as present in, yet different from, what we actually experience. Those ideals are definitely at work, but we must not let our desire to fulfill those ideals cloud the realities of our lived-experience.

In short, it is essential that the ideals, norms, codes, and meanings through which we make sense of ourselves as sexual beings be made explicit in our study of sexuality. These must be examined as semiotic forces that are *both constraining and enabling* in what and how we come to experience sexuality. It is very important that we examine these ideals and norms of sexuality as such, rather than allow them to remain taken for granted and presumed as an accurate understanding. We must, in other words, be willing to see and understand how our culturally and socially based presuppositions about sex and sexuality are at work in the immediacy of our lived-experience. In order to do this we must make those presuppositions explicit. Making those presuppositions explicit creates a shared understanding among us about sex and sexuality that does not directly disclose anything about our personal experience. As we get more comfortable and adept at understanding our presuppositions about sex and sexuality, it becomes easier to talk about our experience, because we have become familiar with our generally shared way of making sense of sexuality.

CLEARING CONCEPTUAL SPACE
FOR THE STUDY OF SEXUALITY

Sexuality is very complex. In order to begin our study of sexuality, we need to make explicit our most commonly shared conceptualizations of it. There are four basic categories that will help us sort out some of the complexities of sexuality: 1) biological categories, 2) social-gender categories, 3) biological-social-gender categories, and 4) categories of sexual practices.

It is important to note that in offering these classifications and their meanings—these codifications of "sex"—I am not suggesting that they are definitive or exhaustive. In fact, it is important that as we review these codifications and their meanings, we come to consider additional and/or different codifications and meanings that remain implicit or excluded in the one I offer below. My purpose in detailing these codifications is to flesh out as fully as possible the various kinds of conceptualizations of sexuality that we take for granted as "knowledge." Our study of sexuality requires that all of our conceptualizations and meanings are posited as contingent, partial, and not ever a final determination. Our conceptualizations must serve a heuristic function that is capable of moving us beyond the initial conceptualizations themselves.

Moreover, these codifications are themselves culturally and temporally specific. Thus, if we find that these codifications make sense to us, it is in large part because we share cultural contexts that allow this scheme to be coherent for us at this particular time. Other cultures have different schemes through which sexuality is understood. I do not present the codifications below as definitive or exhaustive. They should, however, be recognizable as generally accurate to our typical of understanding ourselves and others as U.S. Americans living in these first decades of the twenty-first century.

Biological Categories

Biology is important. We are organic beings. As such we live interdependently with our physical environment, and our biological makeup is a powerful factor influencing our lives. It is important that we reflect on our own understanding of our biological selves, but *not* in an effort to determine cause and effect relationships between genes or DNA and our behavior. Rather, we must recognize that our *bodies are very real physical objects* that are central to our self-understanding because they locate us within a physical, social, and cultural environment that attaches specific meanings to specific bodies, their appearance, their movement, their change over time. Our physical bodies have physical limitations. Our bodies are an essential element through which we understand ourselves and our world. Consider how you felt about your body as a child, then as you went through puberty, and as you feel about your body today. As we consider the kinds of meanings biological categories provide for our sense-making, think carefully about your own relationship to and understanding of your physical and biological self. Under this category we will consider the following three terms: male, female, intersex.

At the most basic level, human beings are divided into two biological categories: male and female. These allow us to understand a male as an infant who is born with biologically male genetics (XY chromosomes) and sex organs (testes and penis) that will lead to the production of testosterone and the development of secondary sexual characteristics during puberty. Similarly, we understand a female as an infant born with biologically female genetics (XX chromosomes) and sex organs (ovaries, vagina, clitoris) that will lead to the production of estrogen and the development of secondary sexual characteristics during puberty. More recently we have come to publicly recognize the category of intersex children as those who are born with ambiguous sex organs that may or may not develop into the normally recognized biology of male or female.

We all recognize male and female as two basic and mutually exclusive categories of human beings from a very young age. The codification of male and female is very simple and total: to be male is to be not-female, and to be female is to be not-male. I suspect that even before we recognize the actual physical differences between our own body and the bodies of members of the opposite sex, we recognize that there are two possible "sexes" and that we belong to one and not the other. As soon as we do recognize the physical differences between our body and the bodies of members of the opposite sex, a vast array of powerful cultural codes and social significations become attached to that physicality. I'm not talking about, "boys don't cry," and "girls are nice." Those are social-gender influences. I'm talking about our awareness of our physical bodies.

Consider when it was that you became aware of your nakedness. At what point did you become aware that everyone must keep their genitals and bottoms hidden, but boys can go without shirts whereas girls need to keep their chests concealed from view? Over the course of our childhood and adolescence the significance we ascribe to our bare chests comes to be radically different for boys and girls, young men and young women (Young, 1990). As we begin to develop a sense of ourselves as sexual beings these physical aspects of our bodies often come to have an ever-increasing significance to our sense of self.

At what point did you become aware, as a boy, that you had a penis and girls did not? What significance did you learn to attach to this difference? How did you understand girls' "lack" of a penis? At what point did you come to learn that girls had a clitoris and you did not? What significance did you attach to that difference? And, for girls, at what point did you become aware that you did not have a penis but boys did? What significance did you learn to attach to this difference? At what point did you become aware that you had a clitoris? How did you become aware of your clitoris? Did your awareness of your clitoris precede your knowing that it is called a clitoris?

At what point did you expect that, as a male, you should be physically stronger than females? At what point did you expect that, as a female, you should ask males for help with physically demanding tasks? Differences in physical strength between boys and girls provide a different twist on these matters because girls and boys are often very similar in physical strength until puberty brings the influence of testosterone and estrogen. In prepubescence, it is common for some girls to be stronger than some boys. If you are a boy and you are told that you must be stronger than girls, yet you see irrevocable physical evidence that you are not, how does that affect your sense of self and your feelings toward girls/women generally? If you are a girl and you are told that you should defer to the "stronger sex" for physical tasks, yet you recognize that you are, in fact, stronger than boys, how does that affect your sense of self and your feelings toward boys/men generally?

These are very important questions to consider because your answers to them reveal important aspects of your sense of self and the social and cultural influences that have helped shape it. Even if we simply limit our discussion of our experience of sexuality to the physical level, we can see that our physical bodies in and of themselves already have a significant impact on how we come to experience ourselves in the ways that we do.

There is one more circumstance that is very important for us to consider. In recent times we have begun to recognize that not all children are born either male or female. We have begun to recognize that—even on a purely biological level—these two categorizations of biological sex are not as distinct or clear-cut as we tend to believe (Fausto-Sterling, 2000). In recent times we have begun to recognize children who are born "intersex." These are children born with ambiguous genitalia that can not be clearly identified as penis/clitoris or testes/ovaries. Unless one does a chromosome test (and sometimes even that doesn't help much) it is impossible to know whether the child will develop the secondary sexual characteristics of a male or female until that child reaches puberty. It is possible that the child has a very small penis *or* a very large clitoris, that the tissues that are apparently "supposed" to become testes come under the influence of testosterone *or* estrogen and develop accordingly. The child's physical sex is ambiguous.

The medical profession has, until very recently, responded to these children as having a "birth defect of unfinished genitalia" (Fausto-Sterling, 2000, p. 50). As Fausto-Sterling points out, the most significant factor in deciding whether an intersexed infant should be a boy or a girl is whether or not the urethra opens to the tip of a "penis" that is large enough for the child to eventually urinate standing up. Yet, even this is ambiguous, because only 55 percent of men have a urethra opening at the very tip of the penis (p. 57). For some men, the urethra opens somewhere along the shaft of the penis. This condition called, "hypospadias," and the condition of "chordee," where the penis is bound to the body by tissue, very often lead to surgical intervention for the infant. As Fausto-Sterling points out, these and other surgeries to "fix" ambiguous or atypical genitalia often require secondary surgeries to fix the failure of the first surgery (p. 62). To be clear, sometimes a surgical intervention is required for the body to be able to function properly. But these kinds of surgeries have often been performed for purely aesthetic reasons—that is, because of our deep-seated discomfort, even fear, of gender ambiguity.

Consider what it might be like to become aware of your body if you were born intersexed. Sometimes parents have the surgeries on their infant child and then hope to never have to mention it or discuss it with the child. Sometimes that is not possible because of the additional surgeries required, so parents find some evasive way to talk to the child about the child's medical condition without making reference to intersexuality or gender ambiguity. It is often the case for these children that, despite their parents' effort to evade the subject, they have some troubling awareness that things are not quite as they appear, and this awareness further complicates what is already a complicated process of maturing into an adolescent and then an adult.

Social-Gender Categories

Our discussion of biological categories has revealed how something as seemingly straightforward as biological sex is, in fact, far more complicated than it first seems. Our discussion of biological categories was meant to make us more keenly aware of the importance of our physical body in our self-perception. No one escapes making sense of themselves from within the cultural codes that link particular kinds of bodies with "healthy" or "unhealthy," "fit" or "unfit," "sexually attractive" or "sexually unattractive," and the like.

It is important to recognize how our discussion of biological categories has made us aware of many of our presuppositions about our own biological selves. This process of making ourselves aware of our presuppositions is crucial and must be continuously engaged throughout our study of our lived-experience of sexuality. As we turn to a discussion of the second basic categorization, *social-gender categories*, we shall see that the complexities and ambiguities of meaning as they are present in the immediacy of our lived-experience become more pronounced, and therefore more difficult to see. Ironically, these complexities and ambiguities are often concealed because we presume that the personality and social difference that appear to correspond to biological sex—that is, masculinity and femininity—are, simply, "natural." It is very challenging, therefore, to suspend our presuppositions about them. Under this category we shall consider *masculinity*, *femininity*, the notion of the *heterosexual nuclear family*, and the notion of the *non-heterosexual nuclear family*.

Masculinity and Femininity

Social-gender categories allow us to understand masculinity and femininity as personality characteristics associated with biological males and females, respectively, by virtue of cultural and social norms. In our everyday lives, we recognize that the characteristics associated with masculinity and femininity may be manifested to varying degrees by both biological males and biological females. I personally consider myself a masculine woman (which does not prevent me from also feeling feminine, and I do), and for all of my life I have very much enjoyed interacting with men in masculine ways. As one of my male karate buddies, who is a very strong and aggressive man, put it, "The difference between sparring with Jackie and other women is that when she's standing in front of you, you know you're going to have to compete." It has never occurred to me that I should consider myself less capable than men in physical activities. That's not to say I haven't recognized the significance of differences in size, strength, and power. Clearly, men are advantaged on those terms. But, skill and competitiveness are not dictated by physical size, strength, or power. Thus, I have always been able to see my own physical talents as talents, and have resisted that notion that I was "pretty good for a girl."

Throughout my life I have had very important and personally satisfying relationships with both men and women. Once I "came out," the quality of my relationships with the male friends in my life were heightened because there was no longer any ambiguity for me about friendship versus romantic interests. My relationships with women who I thought were heterosexual, however, became more complicated because it felt more important to gauge how accepting and comfortable they were with my sexual orientation. My relationships with women who shared my sexual orientation were often more difficult because we tended to presume a certain alignment of understanding simply because we were both gay. That simple presumption seemed to have made some relationships very difficult for me and many others, especially among those of us who sought community based exclusively on the fact of shared sexual orientation.

Both men and women have been very important mentors in my life. I am very pleased to have both men and women in my classes, and I think that my own sense of gender ambiguity allows me to connect with a wider variety of students. My experience tells me that students from across a wide spectrum of differences often feel like I listen and understand where they are coming from.

Unfortunately, the relative ease with which I have been able to embrace and express my masculinity is generally not so present for men who consider themselves feminine (which does not prevent them from also feeling masculine). This difference in the way our social and cultural norms dictate the range of masculine and feminine characteristics, as they are correlated with male and female bodies, begins to open our way to understanding just how powerful our social-gender norms are in constraining how we experience and understand ourselves. This difference also bears a strong relationship to sexuality in that our understanding of the difference between masculinity and femininity (and all of the social and cultural codes entailed therein) very much dominates our understanding of the distinction between heterosexuality and homosexuality. As I have already suggested, the heterosexual/homosexual distinction is utterly inadequate as a distinction that can reveal anything substantial about our lived-experience of sexuality. But, because these distinctions between male and female, masculinity and femininity, heterosexuality and homosexuality are so deep-seated in our social and cultural norms, it is imperative that we see how they are present themselves as "natural" and therefore become unquestionable presuppositions that are very much at work in our ordinary and taken-for-granted ways of seeing and making sense of our experience.

Consider when you first became aware of yourself as masculine or feminine. Can you recall the first explicit messages you received telling you to "act like a man," or that "ladies should . . ."? How did your reception of that message coincide with your own sense of how you wanted to express yourself? As you grew up through adolescence and into young adulthood, how did your feelings about yourself as masculine and/or feminine develop or change? What pressures did you feel to express yourself in particular ways because you were easily recognized as male or female? Left to your own devices, how would you have expressed yourself? For some people, everything in their life and everything they feel within them coincides so as to never provoke self-reflection concerning their own sense of socially based gender expectations in relation to how they understand themselves. For people who find this correspondence between socially based gender expectations and their own sense of self, the ground toward a clear and definitive sense of self is relatively straightforward, unambiguous, and without much struggle.

Consider, in contrast, those people whose lives present them with conflicts between how they are supposed to express themselves and how they actually feel like expressing themselves. These people's lives are often characterized by a great deal of self-reflection and a very active process of learning to read social cues that convey the appropriate and expected behavior. There is a benefit that comes with this circumstance. The benefit is in how the recognition of conflict between social norms or expectations and their own experiences of themselves put them in more direct contact with themselves, with what they see, how they see, what they feel, want they want, what the social world is telling them, and what is possible outside of those social norms. But, this can be a very difficult road to travel, and our normal human tendency toward health and well-being can become distorted in ways that lead to a life with much confusion and pain. How do you understand your own self in relationship to your awareness of social and cultural norms? Think about the things in your life that have come easily, and those that have not. How have those things impacted your sense of self and what you want for your life?

Heterosexual and Nonheterosexual Nuclear Family

I also include the notion of a *heterosexual nuclear family* and *nonheterosexual nuclear family* under the social-gender category. A heterosexual nuclear family is, basically, a male and female couple who have married, who practice exclusive sexual monogamy, and produce and raise children. The notion of the heterosexual nuclear family clearly informs much of what we take for granted about what an adult sexual life should look like. Not only does "family" immediately signify the production of offspring, it remains the most legitimate or socially sanctioned site for sex between a man and a woman. Currently, as far as I can tell, there is no socially sanctioned site for sex between men or between women.

For people who do not want to produce or raise children, who do not want to practice sexual monogamy, and/or who are not interested in having sex with a member of the "opposite sex," the prescriptions of the "heterosexual nuclear family" remain the social norm around which they must navigate their own interests and desires. This is what it means to say that a society is "heteronormative" because everyone in the society is subjected to these prescriptions as the only way to develop a legitimate adult sexual life. If you do not follow these prescriptions or have hopes and desires for sustained human connection like we have with "family" without being heterosexual, married, or interested in producing and raising children, then your sexual life is in some way problematic.

If you are a person, for example, who has never had an interest in having children, then you are aware that you are in violation of our social expectations. This violation is particularly strong for women of child-bearing age. The demand that men "settle down" and raise a family is one that most single men encounter fairly regularly. Male and female couples, especially those who are married, are expected to want to bear and raise children. Those who do not are very aware of those social expectations.

These social expectations have lessened to some degree over the past few decades. That is why it is important we include the category of non-heterosexual family. Today, single moms and women who bear children out of wedlock are not stigmatized like they were only a couple of generations ago. Men and women who couple and have children but do not marry are also fairly common. The advance of medical technology and things like "sperm banks" means that the choice to become pregnant is much less dependent on being coupled, or, for those who have the financial resources, on having the physical capacity to procreate. Adoption is also becoming more socially recognized and less concealed as a way of producing a family. It is not difficult to imagine that, in the United States today, the percentage of people who practice exclusive and life-long monogamy (are virginal until married, or who remained married and faithful to their marriage partner) is relatively small.

Consider your own hopes and desires for your adult sexual life. Is the idea of getting married and "having a family" something you feel strongly about achieving? Have you presumed that you would get married and have children, but haven't really thought about it since you're not at that age yet? What is your experience of being a child, of your childhood family, and how does that impact what you aspire to in your adult life? It is important for us to consider these questions in order to help make explicit our own taken-for-granted presumptions about what our adult sexual life should be.

Biological-Gender-Social Categories

When we combine biological and social-gender categories we begin to grasp the full degree of ambiguities within and among all of these categorizations. The increased visibility and recognition of transgendered and transsexual persons has created greater conceptual space through which to consider the very complex relationship between our biological and social existence. Our rapidly advancing ability to surgically intervene and radically reconstruct our physical bodies has made this complex relationship between our biological and social existence ever more apparent. "Reassignment" surgery, in which one physically alters the body to shift from one sex to the other, makes it possible for people to make a full transition wherein they become easily recognized as the sex opposite of their birth.

As we recognize the growing numbers of people in our society who make successful transitions from transgender to transsexual by completing "reassignment surgery," it is important that we also recognize how much this trend is connected with similar practices that have become commonplace within our general population. For those who have the financial resources, procedures like breast enhancements become choices that girls contemplate from the earliest stages of puberty. Indeed, over the past few years I have noticed a marked shift in the way the young women in my class talk about their breasts. The possibility of having their breasts altered seems almost as inevitable as deciciding how much cleavage to show. Among the women who have had breast surgery in my classes, the two most common reasons are because their small breasts left them feeling like they hadn't reached full womanhood. The completion of breast enlargement surgery allowed them to feel that they had. The second reason is to reduce sagging of breasts after childbirth and nursing. The sagging of breasts seemed to take away from their own sense of youthfulness. The surgery allowed them to experience their breasts as corresponding to their felt age. The advances in medical procedures and increasing availability of these and other surgical procedures reflects a society that takes the aesthetic standards of our time as an appropriate rationale for medically intervening in order to change one's physical body.

A transgendered person is one who by all biological facts and outward appearances is clearly identified as one or the other sex but feels within him or herself an inherent misalignment with that sex. A transgendered person often feels as if "trapped in the wrong body." This inherent misalignment may be clear and powerful to the child from a very young age, or it may be more subtle, expressing itself as an unease that one can push aside depending on the time and circumstances. A young boy, for example, may love to play "dress-up" and other typically "female" games. Such a child may prefer playing with American Girl dolls rather than G.I. Joe, and take every opportunity he can to wear feminine clothing and makeup. The family will easily recognize this child's behavior as sex-gender inappropriate, but depending on the attitudes of the parents, this behavior may be accepted—perhaps even supported, or discouraged—perhaps even punished. Some parents make sense of their child's behavior as a "phase" and expect him to develop more sex-gender appropriate behaviors as he grows. Other parents have a more extreme response that is often rooted in a fear that the child will "become homosexual." This fear can lead parents to punish the child's behavior, and as a result the child learns very early and powerfully that is it bad for him to be openly and freely self-expressive.

In this scenario, the parents' fear aligns with the most negative consequences of a heteronormative culture. These negative consequences mean that any human expression which does not align within a strict understanding of sex-gender appropriate behavior is bad, degenerate, deviant, evil, dangerous. It is in this way that male homosexuality comes to occupy one of the most derided positions within culture. It is from this basic presumption that homosexuality (especially among men) becomes associated with criminality, and from there the jump to presuming that homosexuality itself is, de facto, injurious to children. This presumption also informs thinking which takes homosexuals to be a predatory danger to all people.

And, it is important to note that persons who are intersexual are unrecognizable in our contemporary social world. Every person must be put in either the male or female category. In this sense, then, the relationship between a transgendered person's biology and their expression of recognizable gender characteristics will be seen as either normative or deviant—he looks like a man and acts like one (although one's biology is not directly discernible). Or, they are seen as deviant—he looks like a man but he's acting like a woman. In other words, the transgendered person is caught in a powerful conceptual reality in which there are simply and only two choices: male or female.

For transsexuals, the situation unfolds differently in that as they begin to physically alter their body by the use of hormones and/or surgical procedures; varying degrees of alignment occur until the point where the transsexual becomes perceived as clearly either male or female. Although this is the explicit goal for many transsexuals, it is also the case that no matter how successful the "reassignment," lingering feelings of being different or not quite what one appears remain. This is not unlike the circumstance of intercultural adaptation—no matter how successfully a person comes to fully adapt to a new culture, and no matter how long he comes to continue to integrate that new culture into his self-understanding, the process of adaptation or accommodation can never really be said to end. One can never take away the fact of his original enculturation.

It is very important to remember that a transgender person is not necessarily "homosexual." A heterosexual male may also be transgendered, thereby eventually becoming a "lesbian." Similarly, a heterosexual female may also be transgendered, thereby becoming a "gay man." A lesbian or gay male couple in which one partner becomes transgendered eventually become heterosexual. Taken together, these cases—transgender, transsexual, intersexual—reveal just how pernicious the biological sex-human nature presumption is. The presumption that one can and should draw a direct line between biological sex and social expressions of gender obscures the fact of variability in human experience and expression as they are essentially bound within the social and cultural norms of our time. The more we obscure these facts of human variability among us, the easier it is to draw sharp distinctions upon which judgments are made that all to often lead to justifications for prejudice and violence.

Categories of Sexual Practices

The final categorization we need to consider is the category of sexual practices. As with all the categories we have discussed thus far, our purpose is, first, to create a common basis for understanding, and second, to examine our presuppositions about sexuality. This categorization is more complex than the previous categorizations and is organized according to the following subcategories: sexual activity versus sexual knowledge; the inadequacy of the heterosexual-homosexual distinction; beyond the heterosexual-homosexual distinction; the reality and significance of sexual violence.

Before we begin developing these issues it is very important to emphasize that the most important kind of sexual practice we must be aware of today is the practice of "unsafe sex." The close associations we often hold between AIDS and gay men, or anal sex and the transmission of HIV, grossly distort the reality of "unsafe sex." All sex is unsafe to the extent that it involves the exchange of bodily fluids. And even though most people would acknowledge that HIV and other sexually transmitted diseases do not discriminate, and anyone can have one of these diseases, such "knowledge" does not necessarily lead people to practice "safer sex." Among young people especially, but certainly not exclusively, the idea that "it can't happen to me" often informs our actual practices, even when we acknowledge that it could "happen to me." Our ability to recognize the very real dangers involved in sharing bodily fluids with another human being, and to also be comfortable talking about sexuality, makes a huge difference in our ability to be assertive enough to address practices of "safer sex" even in the most consuming moments of sexual passion. Our ability to do this can translate literally into life or death.

We commonly think of sexual practices, as they are defined by social science research, as things that we do or think and which can be reported or observed. There are many questions we could pose about sexual practices using a social science approach. A social science approach could study things like patterns concerning the frequency of sexual intercourse, frequency of cunnilingus, frequency of fellatio, frequency of anal sex, frequency of masturbation, frequency and number of orgasms, frequency of casual or anonymous sex, frequency of faithfully practiced serial monogamy, frequency of secreted sexual partners, frequency and kinds of sexual fantasy, frequency of acting upon sexual fantasy, number of sexual partners, biological sex of sexual partners, gender characteristics of sexual partners, use of sexual aids including toys and pharmaceuticals, preferred time of day or night for sexual activities, preferred locations for sexual activity, and so on.

All of these questions would produce interesting results which could provide a great deal of information about what people *do* sexually. The difficulty with the social science approach, however, is that it can not examine, except by inference, actual *experience* or the *meaning* we come to ascribe to our experience. The social science researcher himself or herself can collect a great deal of data, but all of that data is at least three steps removed from the fact of experience itself—the thing studied is presumed to exist as a coherent articulation of human behavior or experience, the behavior is observed or reported, the researcher interprets the data generated. The relative significance of the data is determined by the collective community of researchers, and interpretations of the relevance of the data for a general audience is always deeply impacted by the social, cultural, and economic conditions of the day (think how much money is at stake in the development, sale, and use of drugs like Viagra).

SEXUAL ACTIVITY VERSUS SEXUAL KNOWLEDGE

In order to study sexuality as it is experienced and made meaningful, we need to begin with a basic distinctions between *sexual activity* and *sexual knowledge*, between what we do that we consider "sexual" and what we know about what is sexual *in our bodies*. This distinction is important because we often assume that the more sexual activity we have, the more knowledgeable we are about our own sexuality. Being sexual with another human being often does lead to greater knowledge about how our bodies are sexual, about what "speaks" sexually to our bodies, what we desire sexually, and how to fulfill those desires. And, there is no doubt that experimentation with a variety of sexual activities will generally lead us to greater sexual knowledge of ourselves.

On the other hand, we generally presume that someone who has no sexual experience, that is, who is virginal and/or sexually abstinent, has no or limited sexual knowledge. This is a mistaken presumption. *Sexual activity does not necessarily mean sexual knowledge, and sexual abstinence does not necessarily mean sexual ignorance.* Someone who is very sexually active, whether with a single partner or with many partners, can easily repeat the same or similar enough sexual activities so that she or he never considers what might lie on the edges of awareness of their body's own sexual desire. Fear can also be an important factor here in that one may be fearful of expressing particular desires that they fear their partner will find distasteful, or worse. A couple who is very sexually active may, over the years, find a mutual "comfort zone" that becomes stale over time. If the relationship dynamics do not allow for openness about sexual desire and fulfillment, then such a couple, if they remain faithful, could, in the end, be more sexually ignorant than knowledgeable in their own bodies. The same couple who is more actively experimental and open in sexual communication may only occasionally reach places of staleness in their sexual relationship. In short, mature adults can be sexually ignorant, and high levels of sexual activity may, in fact, be closely related to a high degree of sexual ignorance.

Now, let's consider someone who is a virgin and who is committed to sexual abstinence until marriage. We generally presume that such a person does not know as much about his or her body's own sexuality because of a lack of experience. We can make allowances for what such a person learns through masturbation. And, the media representations of sexuality allow a certain amount of knowledge about our body's sexuality to the degree that we recognize our own sexual responsiveness. But, here's the point: our sexual-self-knowledge cannot be ascertained by sexual activity or lack of it alone. Our sexual self-knowledge can only be ascertained reflectively by being in attentive communication with our bodies. Attentiveness to the "knowledge" conveyed through our relationships with peers, sexual partners, familial expectations, and so on, does not necessarily lead to becoming a sexually self-aware human being.

This point was made crystal clear to me by the work done by a particular student in the same class as the extraordinary young man who disclosed his experience of being sexually abused by an uncle. This other student, a female of Filipino descent (both parents had immigrated to the United States as young adults) in a very conservative religious family, talked in class and wrote about her experience standing naked before a mirror exploring her body. It was obvious that this student was faithful to her family's values—clearly, she was not in rebellion, and spoke with respect about her family's attitudes about the proper place of sex—but was also unconflicted about her body's sexual sensitivities. This young woman was a larger, full-bodied woman, her skin was on the darker side, and she did not wear makeup. It has been my experience that women generally, but especially larger, full-bodied women often feel conflicted about their own bodies and their social-sexual attractiveness. Many women have difficulty looking at themselves naked before a mirror, much less using the mirror as an aid for self-exploration. This student's description of her own experience allowed all of us in the class to understand that our usual presumptions about who and how one is sexually self-knowledgeable must be made explicit and questioned.

The point of this discussion regarding the difference between sexual activity and sexual knowledge is that we must not make assumptions about each other's experience or knowledge regardless of their apparent "sexual" appearance. Think about it. Imagine a typical college classroom of thirty or so students. Some of your peers will have a certain "sex appeal" that seems naturally to signify sexual self-knowledge. Others will appear less overtly sexual, and you may think of them as not sexually "accomplished." And there may be some students who seem to have no sex appeal at all, and on that basis it is easy to presume that they have no sexual experience or knowledge. If we allow ourselves to retain these initial presumptions about each other, then we will fail miserably to benefit from the differences among us in our collective study of sexuality.

THE INADEQUACY OF THE
HETEROSEXUAL-HOMOSEXUAL DISTINCTION

Similarly, it is important that we not make the presumption that everyone in the class is heterosexual unless they fit our stereotype of what a gay man or woman looks and acts like. We must be aware of just how prevalent our presumptions about heterosexuality are. And we need to be clear that the stronger our presumption of heterosexuality, the stronger our presumption of homosexuality. In other words, if the only time we perceive the possibility that someone may be other than heterosexual is when they display what we take to be obvious or stereotypical signs of homosexuality (i.e., an overtly feminine male, or an overtly masculine female), then the more strongly our understanding of sexuality itself is governed by this basic, yet deeply flawed and deeply limited distinction.

To "know" that someone is heterosexual or homosexual is to in fact know very little about the person. If one were to consider the differences, just in terms of sexual practices, among heterosexuals, it becomes obvious that to know that someone is heterosexual tells us very little about their sex lives, or even their sexuality. Even a cursory examination of all the possible variations in sexual practices among human beings reveals that variations in sexual practices among heterosexuals can be far greater that those between heterosexuals and homosexuals. What one can "do" sexually varies just as much between heterosexuals as it does between homosexuals. Couples who share a commitment to exclusive and long-term monogamy as part of a consciously shared plan to raise children together have very much in common regardless of the sex/gender makeup of the couple. Among these very same couples, there will be some for whom the conscious commitments they make come to be at odds with their desires, and they violate their commitment to their partners and family. Among heterosexuals and homosexuals alike, there are those for whom the idea of monogamy is at odds with their sexual desire, and they struggle in varying ways to negotiate the social presumption of "exclusive lifetime couple-hood."

Moreover, it is often presumed that for heterosexuals penile-vaginal intercourse is the definitive sexual act. But, the moment we begin looking at exactly how it is that a particular sexual act fulfills a particular sexual desire, it becomes clear that it is not just or only penile-vaginal intercourse that fulfills desire. Rather it is a variety of sequences of acts, an entire context of thinking and feeling in which that single act *may or may not* be the penultimate moment of sexual fulfillment. Orgasm, as a physiological response, may not mark the ultimate fulfillment of sexual desire. Also, consider how the act of penile-vaginal intercourse is different for the couple trying to get pregnant, for the couple who has been unable to get pregnant, and for the couple not wanting to get pregnant. These points simply scratch the surface of things to consider, and point the way toward many more presumptions that we need to examine about sexuality and sexual experience.

Once we recognize the complexity of heterosexuality and the limits entailed in understanding heterosexuality as defined by penile-vaginal intercourse, we can begin to see why the heterosexual-homosexual distinction limits our ability to understand sexuality as it is experienced. Whereas we generally take penile-vaginal intercourse to be the definitive act of heterosexuality, when it comes to homosexuality we generally take penile-anal intercourse to be the definitive act. The first thing we have to observe about this "definition" of homosexuality is that it *excludes* all female-female sexuality, and it *does not exclude* heterosexual sexuality. Moreover, not all male sexual partners feature penile-anal intercourse as the penultimate act of sexual fulfillment. Among some male couples it could be that the question of penile-anal intercourse is less presumed than penile-vaginal intercourse in presumed among male-female couples.

Another presumption entailed in the heterosexual-homosexual distinction is that there are two basic kinds of sexual attraction: opposite sex attraction and same sex attraction. On the surface this distinction seems to hold true. It seems pretty clear that some people prefer to have sex with people who have male anatomy and other people prefer to have sex with people who have female anatomy. But, once we begin considering our experience of sexuality, we see that even this is not so clear-cut. Consider the fact that many people who come to prefer sex with members of the same sex have also, sometimes for most of their lives, enjoyed sexual activities with members of the opposite sex. Likewise, many people who prefer sex with members of the opposite sex have also imagined or actually engaged in sexual acts with members of their same sex. One may prefer an opposite sex partner, but enjoy watching or reading about erotic liaisons between same-sex partners, or, the reverse. Erotic energy, whether displayed on screen or in the immediacy of our lived-world, seems to generate erotic energy regardless of the particular anatomy or preferences of the persons involved.

It is not enough to simply include the category of "bisexual," although there might be some descriptive accuracy to this category. Rather, we must focus on how it is we come to a sexual self-awareness wherein we shift from the presumption that we are heterosexual to recognizing that something with that presumption is inadequate or amiss. While it is true that some people become aware of same-sex sexual attraction from a very young age, for many others that awareness comes later in life. Often, it takes time and experience to become attentive to our body's sexual desires because we all tend to shield ourselves from seeing parts within ourselves that lie outside of the socially sanctioned norm. The situation is similar in kind, though not degree, to heterosexuals whose maturity into an adult sexuality brings a sexual self-awareness that moves well beyond the presumptions they had about themselves as they were adolescents. In short, our sexuality changes over time and with experience. Too often we presume that sexuality, sexual desire, and sexual fulfillment are static things that we know to be as true today as they were when we were born and as they will be until we die.

Beyond the Heterosexual-Homosexual Distinction

Once we recognize and move beyond the limits of the heterosexual-homosexual distinction, it becomes possible to look more directly at our own and others' experience of sexuality because we have loosened the hold that these deeply internalized labels have on our reflective capacity. It becomes more possible to see the details of sexuality, rather than understand it first and foremost within a mutually exclusive binary code whereby one is either heterosexual or homosexual. Once we begin looking at the details of sexuality freed from the constraints of the either heterosexual or homosexual code, we can see more fully the range of combinations and possibilities that are present when human beings seek fulfillment of sexual desire. It also becomes possible to pay closer attention to the specifics of our efforts to fulfill sexual desire as we negotiate the pressures exacted by social codes and norms through which we come to ascribe meaning to our actual experience of sexuality.

Consider what attracts you to another human being. Think beyond an explicit sexual attraction. Generally speaking, what do you find attractive in human beings? Consider the people in your life now. As you reflect on your relationships with the people in your life now, consider those with whom you feel some kind of innate "pull" or attraction whereby you simply enjoy being in their presence. It is sometimes easier to recognize this "pull" or attraction by considering those people with whom you have an aversion. What makes the difference for you between those people with whom you feel an attraction and those with whom you feel an aversion? Now, consider the gender characteristics of these people in your life now. Not their sex, as in male or female, but their gender characteristics as in "masculine" and "feminine." What leads you to love another human being? How does that "love" take shape? To love someone in a sexual way is often different from loving someone in a nonsexual way, but there can also be an ambiguity here where the difference between sexual and nonsexual attraction blurs.

To move even further on this issue, consider what parts of yourself are more easily expressed with these different people. Sometimes what attracts us to other people is what they allow us to see and express in ourselves as much as it is what we see in them. It is probably the case that even these short and simple questions lead you to reflect on many complex and inter-related factors at work in your relationships with the people in your life. The moment we begin to grasp the full complexity of what is at work in our attractions, the more able we are to examine directly the fact of our experiencing ourselves as sexual beings and understanding how we have come to make that meaningful to ourselves in the ways we have.

People who have struggled with their sense of themselves as sexual beings have often had to consciously confront the questions posed above throughout their lives. People who recognize that their own attractions to others involve desires or expressions that are not within what they recognize as the social norms must consciously consider how to manage their desires and expressions within those social norms. In many cases, this means that people who have struggled in this way are much more aware of both their own desires and the social norms through which they must manage the outward expression of those desires. Taking the heterosexual-homosexual distinction as an adequate basis for understanding one's sexual self can limit the kind of reflective examination that allows one to adjust his own thinking and acting according to the actual pleasures, comforts, and dissatisfactions experienced during sexual activity. The ability to reflectively consider one's experience and respond in ways that are faithful to desire allows one to cultivate a full and mature sense of one's desire.

THE REALITY AND SIGNIFICANCE OF SEXUAL VIOLENCE

I have labored much on the inadequacy of the heterosexual-homosexual distinction because it remains a potent framework through which a very basic and simplistic understanding of what is "good" and "bad" about sexuality is sustained within our cultural world. There is no doubt that "bad" sexuality circulates freely in our society. We have good reason to be concerned that in calling for each of us to become faithful to our sexual desires, we could, in fact, be encouraging those whose sexual desires involve the exploitation, degradation, or harm of others. This is an important point that we must address directly through a careful examination of the terms and conditions through which the pursuit of one's sexual desire results in harm to others. The heterosexual-homosexual distinction fails in every regard to assist us in addressing this very important point.

Throughout this chapter I have emphasized the importance of examining our presuppositions concerning sexuality. There are two presuppositions, however, that we shall *not* suspend in our study of sexual experience. The first is that, *in its mature forms, sexuality and sexual desire are inherently good.* We must still, however, be attentive to the ways in which sexuality and sexual desire remain immature and become mechanisms of human degradation or exploitation. It is precisely because sexual desire is often used and experienced in very negative, harmful, and violent ways that we must take very careful consideration of when and how that happens.

The second presupposition that we shall *not* suspend is that any and all sexual activity between an adult and a child is harmful and cannot be condoned, explained, or justified in any way. Pedophilia is a form of immature sexuality that is, in every case, criminal. Statutory rape laws exist for good reason, and although we see the difficulties of applying such a law in a case where consensual sex is engaged in between two teenagers, one of whom is just short of sixteen years of age and the other is just past eighteen years of age, we must also recognize that "consensual sex" between a person who is under sixteen years of age and one who is middle-aged is suspect.

The issue of "consent" is a very important issue that we must look at carefully. It is not uncommon for college students to "stumble" into sexual situations and end up allowing a sexual encounter to continue despite not wanting it or seeking it out. Peer pressure can be very strong in late adolescence and early adulthood. What does "consent" mean if one pursues sexual activity only because one's peer group expects it? We must look at these questions very carefully.

CONCLUSION

To make a direct study of our experience of sexuality as the primary and sustained goal in a college classroom demands a mature, deeply respectful, and open classroom environment in which a sense of our own human dignity can flourish. Our effort to study our lived-experience of sexuality must begin with a thoroughgoing and direct examination of the conceptual schemes through which we make sense of our experience. We must, in every case, be willing to examine the latent or tacit presuppositions informing our thinking no matter how "right" we think we are in our understanding.

My experience teaching Communicative Sexualities to undergraduates over the past several years provides strong evidence that students today appear less "hung up" on issues related to sexuality than previous generations. Issues related to premarital sex, pregnancy outside of marriage, birth control, bisexuality, homosexuality, and so on, do not seem to cause as much concern as for students of previous generations. Women tend to be more comfortable in asserting themselves sexually, and men seem to be less constrained by stereotypically masculine attitudes. Yet, my experience over these past several years has also revealed to me that however "open" these students are in their attitudes toward issues related to sexuality, they retain deeply held tendencies working beneath their level of self-consciousness to retain more "traditional" sexual attitudes even though they would not publicly embrace those views.

I have come to see an ironic "truth" about our apparent "openness" regarding sexuality: the more we claim "openness," the less we think we need to pay attention to, much less examine, our own taken-for-granted presumptions about it. A gap emerges whereby we have a certain idea about how we understand "sexuality," yet in our own practices we are governed by structures of thinking that are sometimes very, very different.

Our purpose in this chapter has been to lay a basic conceptual framework from which we can consider the great variety of sexual attitudes and practices among people and cultures. Our ability to recognize this great variety of sexual attitudes and practices then allows us to reflect on our own experience and desire and come to a clearer understanding of how we have come to have the attitudes and experiences we have, and become more fully attuned to how they have changed throughout our lives, and even from moment to moment. In developing the ability to more fully reflect on and understand ourselves as sexual beings, we can also come to greater awareness about our intimate relationships and what has made them more or less fulfilling.

FOR FURTHER READING

Simone de Beauvoir, *The Second Sex*, trans. H. M. Parshley. (New York: Vintage Press, 1989/1952).

Linda Martín Alcoff, "Phenomenology of Racial Embodiment," in *Visible Identities: Race, Gender, and the Self* (Oxford: Oxford University Press, 2006), 179–94.

Iso Kern, "Intersubjectivity" in *Encyclopedia of Phenomenology*, ed. Lester Embree et al. (Boston: Kluwer Academic Publishers, 1997), 355–59.

3

History, Time, Context

When I was growing up, I presumed that I was heterosexual, and that like all other girls I would grow up to marry a man and have children. The social world I lived in at the time didn't provide me with any way to understand myself other than as heterosexual. I was a very athletic tomboy who knew that my interest in playing sports with the boys was an oddity among my peers. I played organized softball and girls' flag football throughout my childhood, and at that time the notion that girls' sports were inferior to boys' was the truth of the day. As I was growing up, I knew that I was different from most girls, but because I was a girl I could not imagine any future adult life "playing with the boys," or centering on athletics. That was the "thinking of the day" when I grew up in the 1960s and 1970s.

I am very thankful today to see so many young girls with opportunities to aspire to athletic achievement well into their adult lives. College scholarships for female athletes were unheard of when I was in high school, yet today it is possible for even very young girls to aspire to a future driven and supported by their athletic talents. There is no doubt that times have changed when it comes to opportunities for young girls and women today, and not just in the sphere of athletics. The last half of the twentieth century in the United States was, without question, a time in which some of our most basic conceptions about what it means to be a man or a woman has undergone some significant changes.

I see young women today seeing themselves as sexually powerful and assertive in ways that most of my peers and I didn't when I was an undergraduate back in the early 1980s. It is, in a way, a true sign of the success of the women's movement and feminist thinking that young women today simply do not see their gender as anything that should stand in the way of their aspirations. There is no question that, generally speaking, women in the United States today feel more freedom to do and become what they want than previous generations. It is a good thing to appreciate the positive changes for both women and men that have come with the loosening of gender norms, but there is also a lot more to the story than that, and what appears obvious at first glance is rarely so clear-cut once we begin a closer examination.

In the previous chapter, I posed questions that called for reflection on our social and cultural norms as we have negotiated them in our experience of ourselves as physical, gendered, and sexual beings. In addressing these questions for ourselves, we have begun looking at the very particular and complex ways of perceiving, expressing, and understanding that have, to a large degree, made us who we are today. By laying a common conceptual foundation upon which we can begin looking at the fact of our sexual experience as it is both enabled and constrained by the cultural codes and social norms of our time, we make it easier to share the particular ways in which each of us has come to understand ourself as a sexual being.

Our purpose in the present chapter is to begin to explore the many transpersonal influences of our culture and history come to bear within us as deep-seated taken-for-granted presumptions about ourselves, others, and the world. We are, of course, particularly interested in those transpersonal influences that come to bear in our experience and understanding of sexuality. In taking up this task it is very important that we pay careful attention to the fact of *history* and the passage of *time* as they impact the very concrete *contexts* and circumstances through which we come to make our experience of ourselves as gendered and sexual beings meaningful. This connection reveals the many ways in which the concrete realities of a person's lived-experience can reflect the realities of many transpersonal dynamics of a particular moment in a collective social consciousness.

THE "THINKING OF THE DAY"

Consider again the personal questions related to when and how you became conscious of your nakedness, of the difference between boys' and girls' bodies, and of how you came to express yourself in light of the social norms of your familial and cultural world. How we have responded to these questions has much to do with the fact that we are all living in these first decades of the twenty-first century. As contemporaries, we share many common referents of our day. September 11, 2001, the wars in Iraq and Afghanistan, the financial crash of 2008, and the election of the first African American president of the United States are examples of shared referents that have become meaningful to us all in similar ways. These shared referents constitute a common history that creates connections among us that operate separately from our own conscious awareness. In operating separately from our own conscious awareness, they constitute a *sedimentation* of possible meanings. This sedimentation is like a depository in which particular kinds of communicative systems and practices are retained across generations of use.

Taken together, this common history that comes from the fact that we share these particular moments in time and space, constitutes a kind of "thinking of the day" that can appear to be timeless and true. That does not mean that we all agree. Obviously, we have many serious disagreements among us as to how we should understand the significance of any or all of these shared events. When we talk about a common "thinking of the day," we are not talking about shared opinion, or a "locked-in" sameness. Rather, we are talking about something much more subtle that surrounds and influences all of us in ways that we are largely unaware. We are talking about something like an *atmosphere* (Merleau-Ponty, 1962, p. 168) that we all respond to in habitual ways without conscious thought. Some people like cold weather, others prefer warm weather. But regardless of which we prefer, we all adjust to the current weather conditions. We may literally experience the same weather or atmospheric conditions differently, but we all respond and adjust as the weather conditions change. This is what it is like to understand the "thinking of the day," as atmospheric conditions that we all respond to.

Generally speaking, the younger we are, the harder it is to recognize how the "thinking of the day" is present in many of our presuppositions about life. This is generally true because in adolescence and young adulthood our projects are directed toward a full grasp of the world around us. As we grow into adulthood we have greater experiences with a wider variety of people and circumstances, and by the time we pursue a college education we are thinking in terms of directing our own path ahead. A fuller sense of knowing the world and our place in it generally accompanies this time in our lives. As a result, we will have a greater tendency to think in terms of self-mastery and clarity about the world we are moving into. There is a certain energy or vibrancy that goes along with this time in our lives, and that is a great asset for learning in the college classroom.

Coming into our own as young adults seeking to develop intimacy in our friendships and potential sexual relationships is often also characterized by a sense that we should, at least in public, display a sense of self-mastery and clarity about how our lives are moving forward and into our future. Even if we are virginal and sexually abstinent, we understand that adult sexual relationships will occur sooner rather than later in our lives, and therefore we sense that our knowledge about it should also be closer to us rather than farther away. The content of that knowledge about adult sexual relationships can vary widely among us, but all of it is most certainly influenced by the massive exposures we have to notions of sexuality that saturate our media production and consumption. Such consumption often comprises the actual content of much of what we can assert as mastery over our sexual self-understanding. Mastery of this sort must be held in suspicion.

As we continue our study of our lived-experience of sexuality, it is important that we come to recognize how the specific influences of the day shape our understanding of ourselves and the world around us. We must become adept at detecting the movement of thought and feeling across time and history. We must be able to recognize differences among us that are related to generation and community. In short, we must recognize *historicity*. "Historicity" refers to our present understanding of the reality and significance of the past. "Historicity" refers to all of the complexities that come with the fact that human beings exist inextricably in *time*. *Temporality*, or the condition of existing in and through the passage of time, is always a present phenomenon which gives a particular structure to how we perceive ourselves, others, and the world in which we live. Therefore, the meanings we come to make of those perceptions are always influenced by the fact that we exist in time (the theoretical implications of this fact are taken up in chapter 4).

Consider, again, the example of my friend who tells me that I am not a good listener. The fact that I may change my way of listening happens only because the *passage of time* allows me to reflect on what my friend has said. In this interpersonal example, we are very aware that it is this particular person whom we respect and care about who is sending us this very specific message whose meaning is very clear to us. Thus, it is very easy to reflect upon it and direct our awareness to our own actions and experiences of a moment, an hour, or a day ago.

Now, consider how this works outside of the very clear parameters of interpersonal communication. Rather than having a clear awareness of this particular person conveying this particular message with this very particular and clear meaning, we might have a sense that our peer group expects or values this more than that, that more than this, or something else. We are receiving messages, but they are not so clear or distinct. Let's say, for example, that all of my high school friends are talking about having sex. I haven't had sex so I say nothing. I begin reflecting on this difference as I perceive it between me and my peers. That reflection may be very conscious, and as a result I come to form the opinion that I am a "prude" and therefore not as "cool" as they are, or they are "loose" and I have better morals than they do, or I am perplexed and I tell myself that I need to talk with my older brother or sister, and so on. On the other hand, that reflection may be less conscious, and I don't form any explicit judgment about them or me, but I begin to feel self-conscious whenever the discussion among us turns to sex and I tend to "freeze up" in my thinking and feeling.

In our ordinary daily lives we are exposed to an incredible amount of information, and yet, only a portion of that will grab our conscious awareness strongly enough for us to actively reflect upon it. The process of sorting through that incredible amount of information is carried on without our conscious awareness and through the influence of cultural and social codes. Because this happens without conscious awareness it is easy to presume that there is no process of sorting through and, therefore, we see what is simply there. If we tend to surround ourselves with people who generally share our way of seeing and thinking, then we have many fewer opportunities to *see how we are seeing*. We cannot become aware of how we are sorting through the vast amounts of information we are exposed to unless we recognize that there are many possible ways of sorting through the very same information.

This rather basic point is easy to understand in the abstract but becomes very difficult to examine as we move closer to our most dearly held taken-for-granted notions about ourselves, others, and the world in which we live. This is the level at which culture works. We can fairly easily recognize differences in, say, political orientation, or one's general philosophy of life, and the like, but recognizing culture and its codes as they are present and at work in the immediacy of our experience is much more difficult. This is in part because cultural codes are widely shared, deeply internalized, and slow to change. Thus, unlike the circumstance where my friend tells me I am a poor listener, the process for becoming aware of how we are culturally oriented is much more difficult to ascertain and reflect upon. Whereas it is easy to see how the passage of time functions as a key factor in heightening my awareness of the way I listen to my friend, it is much more difficult to see how the passage of time affects our cultural dispositions that frame our very processes of perception and meaning construction. Generally speaking, the younger we are, the more difficult it is to develop these kinds of sensitivities.

I believe that it is also true, unfortunately, that many young people today are startlingly unaware of history—especially twentieth-century U.S. American history. I am troubled by the fact that I have all too often encountered students who literally cannot explain the history of the "n" word relative to generations of African Americans in the United States. The middle decades of the twentieth century, marked as they were by the struggles led by Martin Luther King and Malcolm X, came to be a time of great change in social awareness in the United States. The passage of the Civil Rights Act of 1964 was the culmination of the work of activists and intellectuals who emerged across generations of African Americans. It is unfortunate, in many profoundly important ways, that of all the great contributors in the movement to end legal discrimination against African Americans in the United States, only a small handful of names are recognizable in our common historical consciousness.

When speaking with students in a more global context I have come to expect that I will have to explain what *apartheid* is and how it functioned as the law of the land in South Africa prior to 1994. As a result, it is often difficult for students to see how the legacies of these histories remain part of our social and cultural landscapes. In light of this, our U.S. American cultural presumption that we live in a place of "equal opportunity," where all people are considered "equal," often simply constitutes our way of seeing, even in the face of direct evidence to the contrary. And because we don't see it as a particular way of seeing, it is often very difficult to become aware of how this particular presumption governs much if not all of our thinking and understanding.

Culture changes slowly, and because of that it can be easy to presume that we, as young people living in this particular time and place, are, for example, "beyond" some of the racial or sexual issues of previous generations. And, there does seem to be some evidence to support this notion. Regarding sexuality, it seems clear that issues related to the broad acceptance of birth control, premarital sex, unmarried couples having children, single mothers, gay, lesbian, bisexual, transgender and transsexual people—all these seem more visible and tolerable today than in previous generations. The ease with which young people today accept these issues suggests that we are, as a whole, less "hung up" about sex and less invested in the heterosexual/homosexual distinction as a basis for judgment of "good" and "bad sex." I think that this is a good thing. But, as I also noted in the previous chapter, there is an interesting consequence to this being less "hung up," and that is that we tend to think these issues irrelevant because we have moved beyond them. To think this way is to think mistakenly because the moment we stop reflecting on these issues, the heavy weight of tradition and culture easily come back into play and we have the ironic situation of people saying, quite sincerely, things like, "I'm not prejudiced; I just don't like being around gays."

To be young adults in college often involves varying degrees of figuring out how one wishes to be perceived by one's peers. To be "hip," or open about sexuality, often figures into that figuring out. This can create a circumstance in which we very much *stop thinking* about these issues and the specifics of how they impact our lives and our perceptions of others because we have set for ourselves our notions of how we want to portray ourselves and be perceived by our peers. It is too risky to question our own self-understanding because it is important to us to present ourselves as having a clear and full understanding of ourselves. This circumstance is more likely to occur for those young people whose knowledge about themselves is consistent with social and familial expectations. For these students, the consistency between their internal sense of their sexual selves and the norms presented by their families and the culture at large means that they do not have to spend much time examining contradictions or inconsistencies. These students are busy reaching for their idea of a full and mature sexuality based on their confidence that their current understanding of themselves provides an adequate basis for the development of happy and fulfilling relationships.

Not all young people, however, feel a sense of consistency between their own internal sense of sexual selves and what their family and culture provide for their sexual self-understanding. This means that for these young people it is very difficult to move directly into a future without a great deal of self-reflection related to sexuality. The truly good news about young people today being less "hung up" on issues related to sexuality, is that it means that those who spend a lot of time in self-reflection about their sexual selves can do so with less fear or isolation. But that is not the whole story, of course. I have observed many, many instances where (upon the beginning of my Communicative Sexualities course) students express a wide acceptance of sexual difference, but then reveal hesitation and discomfort in their behavior when one or another of their peers takes that openness seriously and speaks frankly about being outside of our cultural norms in one way or another.

THE PULL OF TRADITION AND CULTURAL NORMS

This is the point we need to understand: No matter what we honestly state and genuinely believe about our perspectives regarding sexuality—especially those perspectives contrary to the norms of our culture—we will all still tend to respond in ways that are more consistent than not with those norms. Let me offer you an example from my own life that reveals this inevitable gap between what we *believe ourselves to believe* and what we *actually believe* as revealed in the way we respond in our immediate and concrete engagement with others.

The example occurred only a few years ago when I was getting coffee at the student union on campus. I had placed my order and was waiting for it to be prepared. It was nearing lunchtime, middle of the semester, and the union was crowded. As I was waiting for my coffee I happened to glance over across the large room filled with a variety of food vendors and a large sitting area, and I saw this relatively large female student standing with a group of three or four other female students who were not large-bodied. This is Phoenix, Arizona, so it is hot, and as is the norm among female students here, the hotter it is, the more skin must show. It is pretty much the norm on campus that when it gets really hot, the female students cover as little of their body as necessary.

So, I'm standing there waiting for my coffee and my eyes fall upon, then stare at, this larger woman who is wearing a halter top and low-rise cutoff jean shorts that expose her midriff and legs in the very revealing way that is the norm on campus. This is a large woman, so the soft and ample fleshiness of her midsection dominates much of her visual appearance to me. As soon as my mind registered this woman's body exposing its bare fleshiness in this way, I responded *reflexively* by cringing. The cringe was my body saying, "Oh, gross!" I literally remember saying to myself, "How could she wear those clothes in public?" My reflexive reaction was informed by a cultural norm which says that women who have full and fleshy bodies are "fat" and "ugly," and that by wearing the clothing she was wearing, she was embarrassing herself and offending everyone around.

My reaction to this woman's clothing was probably similar to the vast majority of people in our society. My reaction was revealing because, unlike the vast majority of people, I have spent almost all of my life consciously fighting against our cultural norms which say that full-bodied women are "fat" and therefore "ugly." Throughout my life I have, like most women in our society, struggled with my body image in terms of body weight and body fat. As a dedicated and practiced feminist, I have spent a great deal of time and mental energy cultivating a sense of women's beauty that is not so consumed by our society's very limited notion of what makes a woman's body beautiful. Yet, there I was, standing right there in the middle of the student union with a reflexive reaction that I personally consider sexist and demeaning toward women. I guess I'm not as "enlightened" as I claim to be. How "enlightened" are any of us, really?

Consider the circumstances of time, history, and context as they were at work for me in this example. I've been examining these issues about women's bodies as they are portrayed in culture and as I see my own body for virtually all of my life. My professional life of some three decades has provided me with formal and sustained attention to these issues. I was on campus, in the middle of my workday and fully involved with these issues as a fact of my everyday work life. If, under these circumstances, I still find myself thinking about women and women's bodies according to the normative standards of our culture, then imagine how difficult it must be for those without such a passage of time and experience. *We have a very demanding task at hand.*

If I am at all "enlightened" about how our cultural norms encourage sexist and demeaning ways of judging women, it is in how I responded *reflectively*, after I recognized my reflexive reaction. Once I realized how I was perceiving this young woman, I was surprised at how strong my "cringe" reaction was. I stopped myself and thought about what I was seeing. I returned my gaze toward the young woman, and this time I saw a *human being*. She was carrying books and a notepad, but no backpack or purse. She was standing with her friends clearly looking around trying to decide where to eat. Her posture was straight, shoulders back, and she was standing firmly on her feet. She was wearing colorfully beaded jewelry around her neck and on her wrists, and her wavy light brown hair was nicely pulled back from her face, falling easily off her shoulders. I wondered what class she was coming from or going to. I wondered how she felt and what went into her making the clothing selection she did. I saw a confident young woman who had a strong sense of herself. And it was only then, after a few seconds of these reflections, that I saw what I have taught myself to see in larger women's bodies—their strength and presence. I am fortunate in that because I have been athletic all of my life, I know the advantages of female athletes who have size and weight. Most of the time when I see a woman's body, this notion of relative strength informs my reflexive reaction. But there was something about this particular setting and clothing choice by this young woman that triggered the kind of response I have actively critiqued and fought against within my own conscious awareness for most of my life.

Later, as I reflected more on this particular experience, I wondered how it was that I could have such a stereotypical reaction when I have so consciously cultivated within myself a different way of seeing. Then I realized it. The fact that this particular young woman was dressed the way she was created that reflexive response in me because I myself would like to be able to show my body in a similar way without being self-conscious. I wouldn't wear a halter top and lowrise cutoff jean shorts. For me, it would be some kind of athletic clothing that reveals every contour if not quite as much skin. I have clothing like that in my closet, but I don't usually have the guts to wear it outside of my house. With this additional reflection I realized how I had pulled a reversal. It was because I have struggled so much with my own conflicting desires about dressing my own body that this woman's body caught my attention as it did. Thus it is that my *reflexive* reaction, which I can only grasp *reflectively*, reveals the fundamentally *reversible* relationship between perception and expression. In the immediacy of my concrete engagement with the social world around me, *what I come to perceive is itself an expression* of my irreducibly intersubjective existence. This irreducibly intersubjective existence is the point at which "the expressive body discloses cultural codes, and cultural codes shape the perceptive body" (Lanigan, 2008, p. 855).

It is this particular point of coalescence *(the subjectivity of intersubjectivity)* at which we must aim in our study of our experience of sexuality. In order to reach into the specific dynamics at work in our irreducibly intersubjective existence, we need to develop a theoretical and methodological framework that is adequate to the task. As we move through this chapter and the following chapters, we shall be developing exactly that theoretical and methodological framework in the form of communicology and semiotic phenomenology.

The point of sharing this example from my viewing of the woman in the student union is to illustrate how our own conscious experience is always situated in time and place, and that the stories we construct about our experience are enabled and constrained by both the cultural codes and social norms—the semiotics—of our time, as they intersect within our own particular interests and sensibilities. Historicity and temporality must be featured in our study of our experience of sexuality, because without them we will not be able to search beyond what we think we know or believe or see to what is actually there in the immediacy of the concrete intersubjective relationships we share with other people and the world.

I stated earlier that I believe that young people today are less "hung up" about sex and less invested in the heterosexual/homosexual distinction than previous generations. The flip side of this being less "hung up," however, is that it becomes easy to stop thinking about these issues because we presume that we have moved beyond them. It becomes easy, in other words, to stop paying attention to how we react to and think about these issues. Once we stop being reflectively attentive to what we experience and perceive, it becomes easy for the heavy weight of tradition and culture to step in and govern our "thinking of the day." I have spent all of my professional and personal life examining these kinds of issues for myself, and still, in that moment of immediate engagement, I found myself responding with those deep-seated social norms of my culture that I have worked so hard to move beyond. We all have a lot to learn about how we exist in the world.

SOCIAL AWARENESS AND CONTEXTS OF COMMUNICATION

It is important that we continue to shift our focus from the fact of our own personal experience and consider our contact with the broader cultural context in which issues related to gender and sexuality have become prominent in our public discourse over the past several decades. It is important that we examine the major features of social awareness as they provide contexts for thinking about the many issues that confront us socially, politically, and culturally. We live in an ironic time in that even while we have made significant progress in countering the effects of sexism and other "isms," it is still easy to find expressions of sexism throughout our social life. We need to consider this ironic situation because it will sharpen our ability to see the complexities of our day. Our point here is to make clear to ourselves the many ways in which the various "truths" of our day contextualize our thinking as experiencing.

The most important social issue that confronted me as a young person was the women's movement. As I was growing up from adolescence to young adulthood I became more and more aware of the women's movement and how issues of sexism affected the lives of all women. Issues related to violence against women, especially rape and domestic violence, were very much in the news. I remember a lot of activism focused on making the legal system more responsive to rape victims so that they would not be victimized a second time by a law enforcement and legal community that was generally suspicious of rape victims' veracity. The "boys will be boys" attitude was critiqued strongly as it became more and more obvious that this attitude facilitated the perception that women who said they were raped were really just asking for it because of the way they dressed or danced or acted, and that it is reasonable that men can't and shouldn't be expected to have control over their sexual impulses. Activism focused on changing laws like those that made it impossible for a man to be held legally accountable for raping his wife. The hard work by dedicated activists of all sorts critiqued the many ways in which sexism was supported and sustained through a wide variety of institutional practices and social attitudes. Young women today who feel the kinds of freedoms they do owe a great debt to those many courageous activists for women's rights who have preceded them. The success of the women's movement has meant that young women today can feel less concerned with or constrained by sexism.

What are the social movements and social issues that you have become aware of as you have moved from adolescence into adulthood? The events of 9/11 must certainly be a primary point of social consciousness. The wars in Afghanistan and Iraq have been present constantly in public discourse and as facts of our social world for nearly a decade. If you are in your early twenties now, then that means that for almost half of your life you have been aware of the difficult, troubling, and complex set of issues connected to these events that we have faced as a country with many and varied communities of people with different religious beliefs and cultural backgrounds. The constant flow of men and women between military service in a war zone and returning home has heightened our awareness of how damaging war is and how difficult it can be to recover from. The wars in Afghanistan and Iraq have also heightened our awareness of our dependency on oil. Issues related to the environment and global warming have taken a particular prominence in our thinking of the day. Recycling as a regular part of our everyday lives is a very recent phenomenon.

A major point in the arguments offered prior to our military interventions in Iraq and Afghanistan was the way in which women are oppressed under the Taliban and within some Muslim communities or societies. It is no doubt true that a particularly virulent type of sexism and oppression is at work when a woman can be legally sentenced to death by stoning for having been raped, or can be legally killed by a male relative if she has dishonored the family. These are important issues that deserve a great deal of study and attention. But for our purposes it is important that we consider how this presentation of the oppression of these culturally-foreign women cultivated our own sense of righteousness toward our own sense of sexual freedom and enlightenment. The point here is not to compare the relative freedoms of women in the United States and women in Afghanistan. Rather, the point is to consider what it is we take for granted when we presume that U.S. American women are sexually free and enlightened.

Much like my earlier discussion about the ideals of true love or romance, it is important that we not let our cultural ideals of "freedom" and "liberty" overshadow our effort to see what is at work when we experience sexuality and make it meaningful in our lives. I am not arguing that we should critique these ideals or abandon them per se, but rather that ideals are ideals precisely because they are difficult to achieve and never fully sustainable. If we fail to recognize the contingency or openness of our own experience by supplanting that with a sense of righteousness of our ideas, then we will live in a state of willful ignorance and denial. We must not presuppose the righteousness of our cultural ideals, not because they are essentially bad, but because they will prevent us from seeing the immediate, concrete, and embodied way in which we actually come to experience and meaning related to sexuality.

Another kind of ideal we tend to hold strongly within our U.S. American cultural sensibilities is an ideal of "nature," or what is "natural." This has often been translated into an appeal to biology or "nature" as an uncontestable basis for categorizing or understanding human beings. This kind of appeal inevitably invokes a hierarchy of values in which some human beings represent a standard against which all others shall be measured as less human or not human at all. The "discovery of the 'New World'" in the fifteenth century, the development of the institution of slavery in the eighteenth century, and the colonial enterprises carried out by European nations and then the United States throughout those times and well into the twentieth century, were informed to varying degrees by a notion that the nonwhite and non-European cultures were comprised of primitive and inferior beings, which therefore made them legitimate objects to be used for the benefit of European man. The legacies of these types of cultural and social beliefs and practices seeped easily into the most mainstream parts of the feminist movement of the latter half of the twentieth century, and provided a basis in which feminism itself, both as social activist and academic practice, became much more attuned to the problems that come with presuming that one's position within a cultural time and place is sufficient for understanding and critique

CONCLUSION

In this chapter I have reflected on the major social issues that constituted my own growing up period and have asked readers to reflect on the major social issues of their own growing-up period. My effort has been to call us all to reflect on the "thinking of our day" and how that has shaped our understanding of ourselves, others, and the world in which we live. As we engage in this process of reflection it is important to recognize that as we live and grow in the immediacy of our everyday lives, we retain and reinforce patterns and habits of thinking and behaving which we have inherited from those who have come before us. Reflection—which is only possible because the fact of temporality allows us to make the past and the future present in the immediacy of our experiencing—is the key action through which we have the possibility of understanding how the major issues of our day have influenced our thinking and understanding.

It is also important that we understand just how challenging it is to actually reflect upon and examine the presuppositions we hold by virtue of living in the times and places that we do. Our own cultural dispositions, which lead us to believe deeply in the ideal of human equality, often make it difficult to see and reflect upon our own hierarchies of judgment related to people different from ourselves. This particular ideal exerts a powerful influence that exists as a taken-for-granted reality expressed in how we see others. It is important to realize that taken-for-granted presumptions are, by definition, difficult to see and move beyond. If we really believe in human equality in a taken-for-granted way, then it is not difficult to see how this very ideal allows us to skip over or ignore evidence to the contrary. My example of my reaction to the woman in the student union illustrates this dynamic in relation to my own ideal of women's beauty.

The point here is to make clear that the work we have to do to make ourselves capable of seeing and suspending our taken-for-granted presumptions is challenging and, often, elusive. This is why we need a more precise and advanced set of theoretical concepts through which we can see, understand, and suspend our own deep-seated taken-for-granted presumptions. We have begun to do this by recognizing the particular "influences of our day" and how these influences themselves emerge from a sedimentation of meanings, habits, and practices that we have retained across generations. Upon recognizing this shared terrain of sedimentation, we also recognize that we exist in an inextricably intersubjective condition that precedes us and sets the conditions for our conscious awareness. In order to be able to examine the presuppositions that inform our most fundamental modalities of seeing and understanding, we must be able to examine those very sedimentations and intersubjective condition. This is precisely the point and purpose of communicology and its methodological expression as semiotic phenomenology. We turn now to a consideration of the specific theoretical concepts that allow us to engage the immediate and concrete realities of embodied experience.

FOR FURTHER READING

Fatima, Mernissi. *Scheherazade Goes West: Different Cultures, Different Harems* (New York: Washington Square Press, 2001).

Lewis Gordon, "Existential Phenomenology and History," in *Fanon and the Crisis of European Man* (New York: Routledge 1995), 13–35.

John B. Brough, "Time," in *Encyclopedia of Phenomenology*, ed. Lester Embree et al. (Boston: Kluwer Academic Publishers, 1997), 698–703.

4

Semiotics in Communicology

When we talk about the "thinking of the day," and the heavy weight of tradition as it prefigures our sense-making and experiencing, we are also talking about the "sedimentations" and the "intersubjective conditions" in which human beings are always and inextricably situated. In discussing these "sedimentations" and "intersubjective conditions," we are pointing to the fact that all of reality, both physical and cultural, consists of *structures* which are directly entailed in our patterns of behavior, performance, and meaning. When we talk about structures in this sense, we should not think of columns that define the shape and dimensions of a building. Rather, we should understand structures more like the structure of an ocean current, or the rhythmic structure of the rising and falling tide. Our emphasis on historicity and temporality in the previous chapter addressed openings through which we can come to see how these "structures"—which are immanent in our thinking and feeling—are part and parcel of the social world and its "thinking of the day" that we know and understand tacitly, without conscious awareness. Sedimentation refers to the fact that to be within the current or rhythmic flow of a social world is to carry over ways of thinking, seeing, and understanding that remain tacit, taken-for-granted, and presumed to be natural, normal, and as they should be. To talk about the sedimentations that carry over across generations and throughout communities is to acknowledge these shared structures that set a juncture of flow and sediment that are the terrain and horizon upon and through which human beings come to the specific consciousness and experience we do.

These semiotic structures and sedimentations, however, do not constitute the totality of what is at work when the specific fact and reality of a particular human being's consciousness and experience emerge. This is because human beings are "condemned to meaning" (Merleau-Ponty, 1962/1945, p. xix). No matter how deep or pervasive these sedimentations are, they alone do not constitute the meaning we come to make of our experience or our lives. We are existentially free because we cannot escape the fact that we make our experience meaningful in the ways that we do. Human beings have free choice. "Free choice" does not mean that the constraints of time, place, and sedimentations are not real, or that they can be disregarded in favor of the power of an individual to ignore or otherwise remove the constraints of the social situation. Rather, to have "free choice" means that however strong the influences, pressures, or limits are within our social world, those are not fully determinative. No particular fact of experience or consciousness is ever fully constrained by the fact of our existence within a social, historical, and cultural world. We must therefore find ways to discover how this complex interrelation of sedimentation and freedom is at work so that the we can accurately and adequately account for the emergence and fact of human consciousness and experience.

We cannot escape these semiotic structures, and they are always at work, both enabling and constraining what is possible for us to think, feel, or experience. The scholarly movement known as "structuralism" is born from this insight and should be given credit for shifting the object of our scholarly focus from things to *relationships* (Lanigan, 1988, p. 160; Holenstein, 1974, p. 29). We can not study meaning or experience as things. The only way we come to create meaning and have experience is through relationships, and relationships of relationships. It is like a woven pattern. No one part of the pattern makes the pattern. Only the relationships among the various parts can make the pattern what it is. Once we begin examining the complexities of human life, we quickly discover that the examination of any given pattern or relationship is inadequate because even at the most basic level of communication, we are already dealing with patterns upon patterns, relationships upon relationships.

As an intellectual movement, structuralism has a history in which different scholars have argued its positions in different ways. From a communicological perspective, the work of Roman Jakobson (1990; Holenstein, 1974) is crucial in allowing us to study exactly how this complex interrelation between sedimentations/structures and human freedom is at work in the emergence and fact of human consciousness and experience. Jakobson's work can be characterized as a "phenomenological structuralism" that lays some of the basic theoretical foundations of semiotic phenomenology (Lanigan, 1988; Holenstein, 1974).

Semiotics can be defined generally as the study of signs and sign-systems (codes). Semiotics bears a strong relationship to structuralism as an intellectual movement in that sign-systems—of which language is the prime exemplar—provide us with meaning structures that set particular kinds of limits and possibilities of human expression and perception that are connected directly to the structures and features of *spoken* language. To speak and listen is very much like moving within a current or a rhythmic flow. Sometimes that current or flow is smooth and easy, other times harsh and violent. Scholars have provided us with specific theoretical concepts that sharpen our ability to step within and analyze these various structures and the dynamic ways they are at work in our communication practices.

In this chapter we shall consider the relationship of diachrony and synchrony; apperception and context; the paradigmatic and syntagmatic axes of language; marked and unmarked terms. Our aim is to provide a set of theoretical tools through which we can focus on the reversible relationship between the "expressive body [as it] discloses cultural codes, and the cultural codes [as they] shape the perceptive body" (Lanigan, 2008, p. 855). In selecting these key theoretical issues I am informed most significantly by the work of Richard Lanigan (1991/1972, 1988, 1991, 1992) and his own central place in the development of contemporary communicology. It is important to keep in mind that the breadth and depth of Lanigan's work is much beyond any singular presentation of it. My effort is to identify and explain the development of a selected set of theoretical issues that will allow me to further our study of communicative sexualities in a way that is faithful to communicology.

To summarize, there are at least three reasons why it is important that we understand these theoretical concepts related to semiotics and communication. First, I have been emphasizing the importance of understanding our *situatedness* or *location* in time, space, history, and culture. These aspects of communication that we will discuss below—diachrony and synchrony, apperception and context, and the paradigmatic and syntagmatic axes of language, marked and unmarked terms—all constitute basic structures in and through which human perception and expression are mediated. These structure are always at work in our communication. They are always influencing our perception and expression. Second, despite the fact that we cannot escape these structures, the fact is that we have movement within them. None of these structures precludes us from altering them in our use of them. Too much alteration, however, and we become unintelligible. Third, and most importantly, as we continue with our study of our lived-experience of sexuality, we will be relying tremendously on language—on speech, reflection, and writing. We will be talking to each other a lot. We will be writing about our own and others' experiences a lot. And, we will be reflecting on, rewriting, and analyzing our use of language and communication with each other over and over again.

DIACHRONY AND SYNCHRONY

Recall my description of my response to the woman in the student union from the previous chapter. I argued that the heavy weight of tradition is strong and often retains significant power in our processes of perception, expression, and sense-making despite our own conscious efforts to assert different ways of seeing and understanding. From a structuralist perspective, we could say that despite my conscious effort to perceive women in a way contrary to the cultural norms within which I was raised, that conscious effort was insufficient to override the deep-seated structures—and the sedimentations carried therein—of meaning through which I perceive the world. From a rigidly structuralist perspective, we would say that it is not possible to effect a change in the basic structures of the cultural and linguistic structures through which we perceive and express ourselves by a mere choice to do so. The shift from structuralism to semiotics and finally to semiotic phenomenology challenges this rigidly structuralist perspective.

Although we are not taking a narrowly or rigidly structuralist approach in our study of our lived-experience of sexuality, we must appreciate the fact of structures as they impact our human capacity for perception and expression. We do this by recognizing that structures do in fact change in ways that are beyond the conscious choice or awareness of human beings. The sounds that make a language recognizable change subtly over time and across geographies. In the United States, for example, we tend to pronounce the word, "schedule," with a short *sk* sound at the beginning of the word. But, listening to a British person speak we are more likely to hear a softer and elongated *sch*. Similarly with Canadians, who tend to pronounce all of the letters of "out," or "about." In the United States, we tend to shorten the sound of the "ou" in these words. You and I may both be born and reared in the United States and thus speak American English, but if one of us is from the Deep South and the other from the Northeast, it may indeed be very difficult for us to recognize each other's speech.

There is no doubt that basic structures of language do change over long periods of time, and by focusing on these changes across generations we can learn a great deal about people and culture, migration and cultural change. To study language in this way, as it has developed historically, is to study language *diachronically*. From a diachronic perspective, the appropriate focus for the study of language is the historical fact of it as a sign-system that connects communities and cultures across generations. The perspective here is that grammar, along with the ability to accurately discern sounds in spoken language, are determinative structures of communication whose features and functions exist beyond any particular human being's capacity for conscious awareness. These features and functions therefore have a universal effect on all people speaking the language. To study language diachronically is to make it into an object that can be studied separately from any given person's use of it. In short, a strictly diachronic perspective is constituted as an "objective science of language" in which "the scientist and the observer see language in the past" (Merleau-Ponty, 1964, pp. 85–86).

There is no doubt that this diachronic or historical perspective toward the study of language is an essential aspect of anything we wish to understand related to human speech and linguistic communication. At the same time, however, we have come to recognize that there is also a *synchronicity* to language and speech that is equally important in the study of communication, culture, consciousness, and experience. It was the work of the Swiss linguist Ferdinand de Saussure that pushed the study of language into a more synchronic approach wherein the study of speech and language in the immediacy of its use became prominent. It was the work of Roman Jakobson and Merleau-Ponty, however, that brought diachrony and synchrony together with a phenomenological emphasis into a dialectical relationship wherein structure does not remain an abstract and absent concept like grammar, but is recognized as a very present and concrete fact in that it is studied as it is taken up in use by the "speaking subject" (Merleau-Ponty, 1962/1945, p. 180; Kristeva, 1984, 1986).

This dialectic of diachrony and synchrony posits what Merleau-Ponty (1964) describes as the reciprocal "envelopment" of diachrony and synchrony. For Merleau-Ponty, we must "return to the speaking subject, to my contact with the language I am speaking," "to language as mine" (1964, pp. 85–86). In Jakobson's terms, we can say that in the immediacy of our speaking we do not have an "objective simultaneity" of past and present, but a "subjective experience of simultaneity" wherein "past, present, and future occurrences can coexist in the subjective experience of time [i.e., temporality]" (Holenstein, 1974, p. 29). For Jakobson, "the value of linguistic data is not determined by factually coexistent data alone [a fact of synchronicity], but equally by temporally antecedent and anticipatory data" (Holenstein, 1974, p. 29). Neither diachrony or synchrony can alone be sufficient for the study of speech and language.

What does it mean to "return to the speaking subject," to study "my contact with the language I am speaking" (Merleau-Ponty, 1964, p. 85)? It means to study language as it exists and becomes discoverable in my expressive body. For the speaking subject language does not exist as an object, but as a *gesture* or stylization through which my speech takes its meaning and intention "without my having to represent them to myself" (Merleau-Ponty, 1964, p. 88; 1962/1945, p. 178). As Merleau-Ponty so eloquently puts it, "There is an 'languagely' [langagière] meaning of language which effects the mediation between my as yet unspeaking intention and words, and in such a way that my spoken words surprise me myself and teach me my thought" (1964, p. 88). It is in this way that Merleau-Ponty develops the notion of the "quasi-corporality of the signifying," through which we understand speech as a preconscious reaching toward, much in the way our body pre-consciously reaches toward the other whom we desire. This is what it means to study "the expressive body [as it] discloses cultural codes, and cultural codes as they shape the expressive body" (Lanigan, 2008, p. 855).

As we do the essential work of studying communicative sexualities—as we speak and listen to each other describe our experience of sexuality—it is important that we learn to become attentive to this "quasi-corporality of the signifying" through which our spoken words surprise us and come to teach us our thought. Groups that have been successful at applying semiotic phenomenology in their study of their lived-experience of sexuality have, without exception, come to see and understand aspects of their own thinking and feeling that they could not have except for their close attention to the immediacy of all that was happening within their group interactions. In short, they were successful because they were able to engage the "quasi-corporality of the signifying." This achievement cannot be planned, and no matter how successful I am at presenting the proper attitude and disposition toward themselves and their fellow group members necessary for success, ultimately it is entirely up to them and what they actually *do* in the immediacy of their shared time and space. Moreover, no matter how clear any one of them is about the proper attitude and disposition required for success, that person cannot make that proper attitude and disposition appear as a group experience. It is always and only after the fact of discovery that the group recognizes the fact and reality of what Merleau-Ponty calls the "quasi-corporeality of the signifying."

An Example of the Reciprocity of Diachrony and Synchrony

When, in previous chapters, I have asked you to consider the moments in your life when you have become aware of different aspects of your body and of others' perception of you, I have prompted you to engage this reciprocity of diachrony and synchrony. During an in-class discussion of breasts, for example, one female student described how her experience of the development of her breasts led to the decision to have breast augmentation surgery. She described how the relatively small size of her breasts left her feeling as though she just never reached full womanhood. On an objective level, her breasts and womanhood had fully developed. In every biological sense she was a fully mature woman. But on a subjective level, and in comparison to those around her, she felt less of a woman because her breasts were small. Let's consider the dialectic of diachrony and synchrony here.

As I was growing up cosmetic surgery was not part of our collective consciousness. Over time, this has changed. Our awareness of the fact of breast augmentation as an easily available choice (given adequate financial resources) allows this student to seek a remedy to her less than full woman-hood by having her breasts enlarged. Certainly there were young women in my time who felt similarly about having small breasts. But because plastic surgery was not so common in our collective consciousness, these young women undoubtedly sought out other ways to enhance their "womanhood."

In this example we see that, from a diachronic point of view, the mean-ing-structure that retains across generations is one in which the develop-ment of breasts signifies the achievement of womanhood. Whether my generation or this student's generation, the subjective feelings are in all likelihood very much the same. From a synchronic point of view, however, our *responses* to this feeling change because in the present we have better and more affordable surgical interventions available. In the immediacy of this contemporary student's life, the limited development of her breasts is contextualized by an awareness of the possibility of a surgical intervention.

But, we can also reverse the terms of the analysis. From a diachronic perspective we can see how the prominence of large breasts as a signifier of womanhood within our culture constitutes a static structural element that is "given in the conscious, 'for us'" (Holenstein, 1974, p. 124) regard-less of generation. We could say, perhaps, that the connection of breasts with womanhood constitutes a fundamental grammar of the meaning of being female. We could, for example, track the gradual changes in this "fundamental grammar" by looking at how the bodies of "cover girls" and female "movie stars" have changed over the past fifty years or so. Even while breasts of a certain size remain the primary signifiers of womanhood across generations, there is difference at work in the synchronicity of how women of a particular time respond to their breasts. Consider the moment in time when "bra burning" was a uniting act for large numbers of women. Or, today, with the proliferation of bras specifically designed for specific purposes (i.e., sports bras, T-shirt bras, bras designed to accentuate cleav-age, etc.). Today's student is largely unaware of these changes, and even if she is, it is difficult for the previous generations' standards to supplant her own. In the immediacy of her own experience, her *response* is different from previous generations, but the fact that she feels the need to respond is not. As students talk and listen to each other it is important to consider various configurations of diachrony and synchrony as they are present in the par-ticular experiences they are considering.

Apperception and Context

The importance of understanding the dialectical relationship between diachrony and synchrony is that it offers us a direct parallel to how we can understand the relationship between our own thinking and feeling of the concrete and immediate moment, and the ways in which our abstract conceptions of things are cultivated from our cultural, social, and familial upbringing. Understanding what happens in this convergence is what happens in all communication and meaning construction.

Diachrony and synchrony are concerned primarily with temporality. *Apperception* is another concept related to temporality that we should become familiar with. Apperception refers to the fact that perception itself always occurs in a temporal context. That is, what we perceive at one moment is affected by what we have perceived the moment before and what we anticipate perceiving in the moment ahead. In other words, the sequence in which we perceive has an effect on what we perceive. Consider these two sequences:

$$12\ \ 13\ \ 14$$
$$A\ \ 13\ \ C$$

The same mark, "13" (synchronic) easily stands for the number "13" or the letter "B" depending on the sequence (diachronic) in which it is found. The numbers 12 and 14 set the context so that "13" is the number 13. The letters A and C set the context so that "13" is the letter B. The same dynamic of apperception is also at work when we meet someone who bears a strong resemblance to someone from our past. We can't help but literally see the person we knew previously in this person standing before us, and we literally expect this person to behave as our friend would. Memories of our time with that earlier relationship come present to us, and even though we consciously resist making these two people the same, we can't help but see (synchronic representation) the new person according to the ways in which we had come to see the person from earlier in our life.

Or, take a slightly different example. I get in my car to go to work and am driving as I usually do. I'm not exactly sure how fast I'm driving because I don't pay attention to the speed limit signs and I don't monitor my speedometer. Then I see the red lights flashing in my rearview mirror. It is a cop. I pull over and I get a speeding ticket. Now, as I continue on my way to work, I am paying very close attention to my speedometer and am on the lookout for the posted speed limits. In this example, we see how apperception has affected my selection of objects within my immediate environment.

These examples reflect another aspect of perception and apperception—both are very much related to *contexts of choice* and *choices of context*. In the first example, the sequence of letters or numbers is completely unproblematic as long as "13" appears with either letters or numbers. But, once we see both sequences, as diagramed above, then we know that "13" could be both or either the number and the letter. If we see "13" in the middle of sequences of both letters and numbers, like a tracking code for a package handwritten on a page, then we may not at all be sure if it

is a number or a letter. In this case we must select the context by deciding if it is a number or a letter. It turns out, of course, that because it is
a simple binary choice we can engage a simple process of trial and error
and determine which reading of the mark is correct. But, in the second
example it is not so easy. If you had known that there was going to be a
cop monitoring the speed of traffic along your normal route to work, you
would have selected your speedometer and posted speed limit signs as
the context for your perception while you were driving. But, you did not
know that a cop would be there so you chose that context for perception
only after the fact of getting the ticket (of course, cops often position their
police cars conspicuously to train us in apperceptive driving, and this is
different from cops who try to be inconspicuous and catch us on radar to
exact punishment rather than training!).

This example also reveals another aspect of apperception: *spatiality*. When
it comes to human perception and expression, the dynamics of temporality
are never separable from the dynamics of spatiality—our lived relation to
space. Sequence can be predominantly temporal *or* spatial, but it is always
both temporal *and* spatial. Because we exist within our physical bodies, the
temporality of sequence can never be fully separated from the spatiality
of sequence. Consider an analog clock with a second hand. The passage
of time is marked by movement through space. As embodied beings, the
passage of time is often marked by changes in our body—changes in body
position or location, and changes in internal body states. We know what
our healthy and alert body feels like and that allows us to notice when our
body feels less than healthy or alert. We recognize that traveling through
the space before us seems quite challenging whereas the previous week it
seemed somewhat easy. As we consider the fact of our lived-experience of
sexuality it is important that we be able to ascertain the particular ways in
which apperception helped structure what came to be.

THE PARADIGMATIC AND SYNTAGMATIC AXES OF LANGUAGE

The paradigmatic and syntagmatic axes of language constitute a basic structure of all human languages. It is important that we come to see how these
two basic axes or structures of language are present and at work in our expression and perception. As we listen to ourselves and each other talk about
our experiences of sexuality, these concepts aid us in seeing beyond the first
most obvious or apparent meaning of the words, and allow us to examine
those aspects of our speaking and hearing that point to the fuller scope
of the expression and perception are imminent, yet never fully contained
in the structures themselves. Speaking, reading, writing, and gesturing all
have a sequence to them that requires the passage through both time and

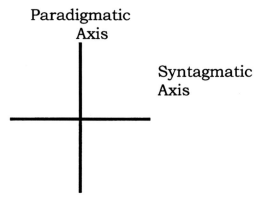

Figure 4.1. Paradigmatic and Syntagmatic Axes of Language

space. All languages are structured according to two primary axes: an axis of substitution (metaphor) and an axis of sequence (metonymy) (see figure 4.1 above).

These axes account for the basic grammar of all languages. In order to be intelligible, speech must conform to a certain minimal structure that can be recognizable by speakers of the same language. We do this by doing two things. One is that we make a selection from a large stock of possible linguistic units, and the other is that we combine these selections into more complex units (Holenstein, 1974, p. 138). Thus, if my friend asks me to describe a work colleague of mine whom he is interested in dating, I then have to select from a wide variety of possible words to describe my colleague. Let's say that I know my colleague to be a very serious and intellectual person who is sometimes awkward in social situations. But I also have come to know him as a very caring and considerate person even though it took me a while to come to see that. At minimum I now have at least five words I can use to describe my colleague. Which one of the five I select could depend on a number of factors, but let's say that I think my colleague and friend would be a good match and I want them to get together. I would probably avoid the word "awkward" and select "caring" or "considerate." Or, if I feel it necessary to include "awkward," the sequence in which I use that word relative to others will make a difference in the overall meaning of my response.

Thus I have two choices to make, the selection of words and the putting of words into a more complex unit, like a sentence. Consider these two possible responses to my friend: 1) "Well, I think he is a generally considerate person. 2) "I know him to be a very considerate person." I've selected the same adjective, "considerate," but the sequence in which I placed it makes

Table 4.1. Paradigmatic and Syntagmatic Choices

He	is	a very	serious	professional.
Mr. Matthew	is	a somewhat	intellectual	man.
Matt	is	an unusually	considerate	person.
My friend	is	a sometimes	awkward	kind of guy.

it convey two very different meanings. The choice of adjective occurs along the paradigmatic axis, and the choice of sequence occurs along the syntagmatic axis. Consider the schema of paradigmatic and syntagmatic choices in table 4.1. above.

All of these descriptions are accurate in my experience of Mr. Matt Matthew. Notice how any of the words in the vertical or paradigmatic axis can be substituted for another and the sentence will be fully intelligible. Whenever we speak, we make selections and create combinations from an existing set of possible things in order to construct something intelligible to those we are speaking with. All of the adjectives above are possible words I could use in response to my friend's inquiry. They exist abstractly in my conscious awareness. But the moment I select one over the other, say "serious" over "considerate," things become very concrete. In speaking the word "serious," I have made something real that will now be relevant to all that I say subsequently. This dynamic of selection and combination are also at work in our practices related to the clothing we wear and the food we eat (Leeds-Hurwitz, 1993). Being able to attend to the range of possibilities of sequence and substitution at work in our speech and behavior is especially important during the phenomenological reduction portions of the research.

Marked and Unmarked Terms

We need to become familiar with another concept related to structure and language: marked and unmarked terms. Our need to understand marked and unmarked terms is because, well, not all words (terms) are created equal. Moreover, because we know that sequence makes a difference in the meaning we make of any given word or utterance, we also know that this relative inequality of words and utterances is very much context and time dependent. As we begin examining our own and our classmates' use of language, we will need to become highly attuned to how our actual use of language is conveying its meaning. This will help us become better at discovering "revelatory phrases," which will be a key element in our application of semiotic phenomenology. The point is, we need to develop the ability to ascertain which words or phrases convey more of the "umph" or weight of the meaning than the others. Consider this example taken from Holenstein (1974, p. 131). Read the two sentences below:

"Peter is as young as Paul."
"Peter is as old as Paul."

Which sentence tells us more? Which sentence gives us more information? Both situate Peter's age in relationship to Paul. Yet, the difference in saying someone is "as young as" as opposed to "as old as" is significant. In the first statement we know that both Peter and Paul are "young," and this means that they cannot be middle-aged or elderly. But in the second sentence we cannot be as sure of either of their relative ages. To be "old" in this case simply means a progression of years. It doesn't carry the signification of youth, adult, or elderly. On the other hand, "young," excludes the possibility of Peter and Paul being older than a young adult. In this example, the word "young" is a marked term because it gives us more information.

In some cases, the difference between marked and unmarked terms reflects a hierarchy of values common within a given culture or community. Consider the heterosexual-homosexual pairing. In this case, the marked term is "homosexual" and the unmarked term is "heterosexual." This is because, unless otherwise specified, we presume that everyone is heterosexual, and thus the fact that we presume someone to be heterosexual does not provide us with any additional information about him or her. "Heterosexual" is unmarked because it does not carry any culturally delimited meanings per se. "Homosexual," on the other hand, carries some very strong culturally delimited meanings. Upon presuming or otherwise assigning the label "homosexual" to another human being, large sets of culturally based "knowledge" about that person are invoked, that is, a context is marked by possible meanings. In our ordinary everyday life, we do not see other people as "homosexual" except for a presumed set of known stereotypical markers of behavior or appearance. Once we see one of those markers, we become immediately aware of the "common knowledge" (all markers) we all know about "homosexuals."

CONCLUSION

Our discussion in this chapter has aimed to provide us with technical terms and concepts through which we understand the many semiotic systems, or structures, within which human beings are inextricably tied. In presenting these terms and concepts, the point was to identify with greater precision the ways in which these structures both constrain and enable human expression and perception.

To study our lived-experience is never as easy as it seems. After all, I am the only one who can say what my experience is, and because it is mine I have direct access to it. Even if we take seriously all that I have discussed about the fact that humans exist inextricably within time and space, culture and history, and that therefore our experience is never just of our own making, it still seems as though once we get to the business of saying what our experience is, well, it's just obvious. The terms and concepts discussed in this chapter will help us develop the capacity to see and recognize the complexity of our immediate experience and move beyond the common and tenacious presumption that when it comes to my experience, I know.

It is very important that we cultivate the capacity to examine the many interrelated factors at work in the concrete and immediate moments of embodiment through which we make sense of our experience. In the following chapter, we turn to a phenomenological emphasis as we begin to flesh out the relationship between the structures and processes considered here and the communicative practices we come to engage.

FOR FURTHER READING

Elmar Holenstein, *Roman Jakobson's Approach to Language: Phenomenological Structuralism*, trans. C. Schelbert and T. Schelbert (Bloomington, Ind.: Indiana University Press, 1976).

Maurice Merleau-Ponty, "Phenomenology of Language," in *Signs* (Chicago: Northwestern University Press, 1964), 84–97.

Richard Leo Lanigan, "Structuralism," in *Encyclopedia of Phenomenology*, ed. Lester Embree et al. (Boston: Kluwer Academic Publishers, 1997), 683–89.

5

Phenomenology in Communicology

Our discussion in the previous chapter emphasized how language and other semiotic systems constitute structures that both enable and constrain human expression and perception. Because of our capacity for conscious awareness, it is possible for us to come to see and examine those very structures as they are at work in the immediacy of our lived-experience. We must simply take this fact seriously and recognize how demanding a task it is to actually do so. Upon this recognition, we can see and thereby use the advance theoretical concepts that aid us directly in achieving this objective of focusing on the concrete immediacy of our lived-experience. It is important to make clear that the work we have to do to make ourselves capable of seeing and suspending our taken-for-granted presumptions is challenging, often elusive, and susceptible to self-delusion or denial. This is so because so much of what happens on a semiotic level happens beneath our conscious awareness. We are busy responding to the people and exigencies of our everyday lives, which have their own complex patterns and habits.

This is why we need a precise and advanced set of theoretical concepts through which we can see, understand, and suspend our own deep-seated taken-for-granted presumptions. We have begun to do this by recognizing the particular "influences of our day" and how these influences themselves emerge from a sedimentation of meanings, habits, and practices that we have retained across generations. Upon recognizing this shared terrain of sedimentation, we also recognize that we exist in an inextricably intersubjective condition that precedes us and sets the conditions for our conscious awareness. In order to be able to examine the presuppositions that inform our most fundamental modalities of seeing and understanding, we must be able to examine those very sedimentations and intersubjective conditions.

71

Phenomenology's contribution to communicology is its commitment to lived-experience. Within communicology, phenomenology and lived-experience are, by definition, intersubjectively imbued. This means that any solitary reflection or pure introspection that aims to situate itself outside of a social context of historicity, temporality, and the sedimentations entailed therein fails in its effort to accurately or adequately detail the complexity of reality as it emerges in the immediacy of our communicative practices. In the discussion below, we shall consider the relationship between phenomenology and human communicative practice and the fact and consequence of living in contingency. This discussion is followed by a detailed description and illustration of Ruesch and Bateson's (1987/1951) four networks of human communication. These four networks and their characteristics can be taken as a fundamental fact of human orientation within a social world.

PHENOMENOLOGY AND
HUMAN COMMUNICATIVE PRACTICE

At this point in our study, we must being to specify the terms and conditions through which we can adequately and accurately examine the fact of our lived-experience of sexuality. Our focus on communicology allows us to more fully appreciate and examine the fact that any moment of any particular conscious awareness is possible only because each of us is *situated* within the complex and dynamic structures of meaning and relationships as they are provided for us by our social and cultural world. As human beings, our existence is fundamentally intersubjective and semiotic. As human beings we are simply and profoundly connected through our mutual location and participation within signs and sign-systems.

This intersubjective and semiotic existence precedes and undergirds the sense we come to develop of ourselves as subjective beings. The intersubjective nature of our human existence renders our typical sense of ourselves as in possession of an "identity" to be fundamentally flawed because whatever "identity" is, it is an ongoing achievement that is *contingent*. As human beings, we are free, and our futures are open possibilities. As conscious beings, we are constantly in the mix of things that require us to change, adjust, and adapt. All of this happens through communication. Communication is the basic constituent of our intersubjective existence. It is through communication that our intersubjective existence enables the dynamic and ongoing achievement that we come to recognize simply as *experience*.

In a purely intellectual sense this is not a difficult notion to see or understand. From the moment we are born, we are responsive to our environment. Through the acquisition of language, we come to recognize complex sets of social and cultural codes carried in both the formal grammatical structures of language and the practical use of speech. We develop the ability to read the codes of emotion in facial expression and body comportment. Our body becomes oriented to its own ability to move through space, manipulate objects, and to the limitations created by the physical spaces we are in. As human beings we never cease being interconnected with others and our environment in these ways, but we often become so adept at living within them that we lose the ability to see that they are there.

It is also true that these complex and dynamic structures of meaning through which we are interconnected with others and the environment can create radical change in how we understand and experience ourselves, others, and the world. Consider what happens when someone enlists in the military. Military training creates structures of time, space, and human interrelations that can fundamentally change the way a person thinks, feels, acts, and comes to experience—otherwise how could killing another human being be made into habit? In a more mundane sense, we can all recognize how taking on a new job or moving to a new and different community affects how we see and understand ourselves, others, and the world.

When it comes to sexuality, these complex and dynamic structures of meaning can exert a very powerful constraint in how we understand ourselves. The experience of "puppy love" commonly portrayed in television and movies of all sorts illustrates how powerful it can be when a young person discovers a convergence between an awakening of heightened sexual pleasure and a feeling of idealization or enamor of another person as an object of love. On the other hand, extreme sexual frustration, or a feeling of powerlessness relative to the object of one's desire, can often lead to hate and a pathological condition of using sexuality to exert control over and harm other human beings. This scenario is undoubtedly at work for many rapists and sexual sadists. The perspective of the one who is the object of pathological sexual desire is especially important in our study of our experience of sexuality. Consider how it is possible that even in the most obvious case of sexual violence, where the perpetrator is clearly solely responsible for the sexual violence, the victim often comes to blame herself or himself. In our study of sexuality, we must be able to sort through the particulars of how these complex and dynamic structures of meaning both enable and constrain us in the very processes through which it becomes possible for us to have had the sexual experience we had.

Living in Contingency

As I just noted, in a purely intellectual sense it is not difficult to understand that we are influenced by the meanings provided to us by our culture. On the other hand, it is very difficult to see how this fact plays out in the immediacy of our embodied experience. As U.S. Americans, it is often particularly difficult for us to shift from an intellectual understanding of how meaning systems influence us to an embodied understanding wherein we can examine the exact and immediate "stuff" through which we come to think, feel, or act in the ways we do. It is difficult for us to understand this in part because our very patterns of perception in U.S. American culture put us at the center, as autonomous and sovereign agents, the sole creators of the meanings we come to make of our activities and lives. By understanding ourselves as autonomous and sovereign agents of the meanings we create in our lives, we severely limit our capacity for understanding the many interrelationships that are essential in the very process through which we come to make experience meaningful.

Because U.S. American culture tends to cultivate a totalizing notion of individuality, it is often difficult to fully appreciate the fact that this notion of individuality itself is created and sustained by virtue of our interdependence with others and our environment. If we do not believe that how and what we perceive is connected to others and our shared environment, then it is easy to believe that it is possible to observe objectively. In our study of sexuality we must absolutely understand that any effort to study, observe, describe, or interpret is never purely objective. Even more importantly, we must recognize that our goal is *not* to describe an "objective reality." That is not to say that there is no such thing as an "objective reality," but that by presuming its existence we actually limit our ability to study it.

Studying our lived-experience of sexuality is challenging in many ways. Even assuming we can create a classroom environment in which everyone is confident in the level of respect and maturity, and feels safe in discussing their sexual experiences, there is still something fundamentally challenging about asking questions that put one's understanding of one's own sexuality into question. To give up the idea that we are fully knowing subjects conscious of our sexual selves can be very threatening. If we come to question our presumptions about the "objective" truth of our sexual desire, or our capacity to fully know ourselves sexually, then we must deal with the possibility of discovering things that are different from what we expect.

Most of the time we expect that as we grow into adulthood and develop a full and mature sense of ourselves as sexual beings, we will discover things about ourselves that are very much in keeping with our own expectations as they have been influenced by our families, peer groups, social world, and culture. We may or may not be virgins before we get married, but the notion that sexual fulfillment should come within a single, primary, and monogamous relationship that lasts for the majority of one's life remains a strong cultural norm. We could consider this norm a "structural constraint." We are all situated within this "structural constraint," yet some of us will be able to find sexual fulfillment within it and others will not. There are an infinite number of ways one could be able or not to find sexual fulfillment within this particular "structural constraint," but we will never be able to discern exactly how we are or are not fulfilled if we are not able to ask the question as to how these "structural constraints" are at work in the immediacy of our own sexual experience. In order to further our study of our experience of sexuality, we must become adept at discovering, then ascertaining the extent of these "structural constraints" as they are at work in the immediacy of our interpersonal and group relationships.

Let's say that I like being in a monogamous relationship, and that I am, generally speaking, sexually fulfilled in that relationship. At the same time, however, I have an active fantasy life, and I find myself having sexual fantasies about particular people outside of my fulfilling relationship. How do I respond to my recognition of my reaction? Perhaps I feel guilty for imagining sex outside of my committed relationship, and I take up the practice of redirecting my thought away from those fantasies and avoiding those situations or people who tend to stimulate them. Or, perhaps I respond by bringing those fantasies into my primary sexual relationship, imagining that my partner is the person in my fantasy. Another possibility is that I could tell my partner about my fantasy and together we construct a way to bring that fantasy fully into our shared sexual relationship. There are many other possible ways one could respond in this situation, and for each of them we could describe endless scenarios for how things unfold. Notice, too, how radically different my experience may come to be, depending upon the particulars of my response. In fact, there are literally an infinite number of ways these scenarios could work out, but all of them would be tied in an essential way to the particular "structural constraints" carried within our cultural codes, which hold that sexual fulfillment should come within a single, primary, and monogamous relationship that lasts for the majority of one's life. In other words, were it not for this "structural constraint," my sexual fantasies about a person outside of my committed relationship would not lead to my having to develop these kinds of strategies for dealing with it.

Networks of Communication in Communicology

The problem we encounter in our study of our experience of sexuality is one of never being able to stand outside of that which we observe. When it comes to human beings studying human beings, there is no such thing as an objective or neutral observer who can stand outside of that which is observed. Not only can we not stand outside of that which we observe, the fact that we are observing changes what we observe. The phenomenological emphasis in communicology allows us to engage this problem of the observer being integral to what is observed with a scientific rigor that does not succumb to the presumptions of an objective reality that can be known separately from the human being observing it.

The study of human communication often focuses on the exchange of *messages* between communicators. Generally speaking, we can say that communication is successful when there is a correspondence of meaning attached to the message exchanged between communicators. Most theories and models of human communication take this notion of correspondence of meaning as the central feature. Communicology is no different, except that from a communicological perspective we always understand that there is no such thing as a message without a *code* and a *context*. From a communicological perspective we understand especially that consciousness itself is central in the constitution of the context within which codes are used and messages conveyed and received.

Some messages are very concrete and explicit. In interpersonal communication, we can ask our interlocutor directly how our message was understood and, through this process of feedback, zero in on a correct meaning with a high degree of confidence. Codes, on the other hand, are not as explicit, and they are often more difficult to discern. This is because in order for successful communication to occur at all, there must be some point at which both communicator and communicatee share the same code(s). If we are speaking, then we must share at least some of the grammatical structure and vocabulary of the same language. If we are playing a game, like baseball or soccer, then all we need to communicate is a common understanding of the basic rules of body and object movement. If we are trying to cultivate love, then success requires that we have common ways of codifying love. The more thoroughly we share the same codes, the easier communication is, and the less we need to pay attention to the codes that allow us to communicate successfully. Codes can become so shared and familiar that we become completely unaware of them. This is the level at which cultural codes work. These codes come to constitute the presumptions that inform our deep-seated and taken-for-granted ways of seeing and understanding. Our habits of bodily comportment are central in the codification of messages and practices of communication. The "language" of body movement makes activities like dance, or athletic contests, communicative in ways that can be much more precise than ordinary language.

In studying our experience of sexuality, we will focus on both messages and codes as they are consciously and preconsciously present in the immediacy of our sexual experiences. We will begin developing our communicological approach to our study by considering the basic characteristics of communication as they occur within four primary levels or networks of communication: 1) the intrapersonal network, 2) the interpersonal network, 3) the group network, and 4) the intergroup network. These networks were first detailed in the work of Jürgen Ruesch and Gregory Bateson (1987/1951). We shall focus on descriptions of communication so as to illustrate how the interplay of messages and codes is at work in the unfolding of conscious experience as they occur within four networks of communication.

In preparation for our discussion of each of these networks, we need to be aware of four basic principles that apply across all of them. First, all networks are always present in our experiencing. Second, our attention will tend to focus more greatly on one or another network, and it is impossible to maintain a single focus on all of them simultaneously. Third, our perceptual capacity is inconsistent. Sometime I am very sharp in seeing the particulars of an interaction, other times less so. For example, we all have had the experience of being so engrossed in reading or studying that we are completely oblivious to what is happening outside of us—I sit in a bustling cafeteria on campus and am so engrossed in studying that I am completely unaware of a loud argument just a few tables away that threatens to become physical. Similarly, I might be fully consumed with worry about a loved one, but someone says something to me I find insulting, and in that moment all of my thoughts of that loved one disappear from my conscious awareness. Fourth, as these examples illustrate, we can shift rapidly from being primarily engaged in one network to another (Ruesch and Bateson, 1987/1951, p. 247).

THE INTRAPERSONAL NETWORK

The intrapersonal network consists of all communication that occurs within a person. Communication at this level is totally encompassing. We are always participating fully in communication at this level, regardless of our degree of self-awareness of that fact. At this level we are fully present to ourselves, although it is impossible to see all that this entails because we can never be fully transparent to ourselves. Self-talk (or "thinking to myself") is an example of communication at the intrapersonal level. I am both the sender and receiver of messages. Both the origin and destination of messages come from within the person, and therefore there is no directional flow of messages. Sending is receiving and receiving is sending. Feedback is impossible because there is no point at which the message is outside of the system of codification. The system of codification itself is impossible to observe directly and difficult to discern. Therefore, the correction of errors in messages and the system of codification is very difficult, if not impossible. Each of these characteristics of intrapersonal communication constitutes a "structural constraint" of what is possible for us to experience (Ruesch and Bateson, 1987/1951, p. 278).

Self-reflection allows us to create an impression that we are able to examine our own system of codification at the intrapersonal level. We can, for example, stop our thought and ask ourselves what we are thinking. And then we can answer ourselves. But that does not constitute feedback or an intervention because the self-reflection itself is based within a system of codification that is fully self-enclosed. Because all four networks are present at all times, it may appear that when we are immersed in deep self-reflection we can become self-enlightened to the point of significantly altering the way we codify our experience. In point of fact, however, self-reflection has this power only because we are simultaneously located within the other networks as well. Because we are first and foremost social beings, what comes to take hold within us at the intrapersonal level is always related to the other networks or levels of communication. The *inter*personal level is particularly important in this regard.

The intrapersonal level of communication makes it possible for us to create "evidence," if you will, that sustains our own perception and system of codification even if that "evidence" is contrary to every other person with whom we communicate. At this level of communication, we can easily reconcile differences in perception between self and other because we are totally encompassed within our own system of codification. It is, simply, how we see ourselves and our world. In our *being* in our intrapersonal world, it is possible that we integrate information from others that can appear obviously contrary to someone else but resides comfortably and without contradiction within ourselves. Consider a situation in which people who are close to us and whom we trust tell us directly that we have produced very high-quality work and have made a great achievement. We hear what they say, understand it exactly, and yet at the intrapersonal level we can maintain a system of codification in which all of those messages are turned into a "yes, but. . . . " Even though we hear, understand, and accept the veracity of the message, we still do not understand ourselves as someone who produces high-quality work or who has made a great achievement. People with low self-esteem cannot be talked into appreciating their own self-value. They must in some way come to experience themselves as valuable.

Another example of this dynamic, and one of its most severe contemporary expressions, occurs with anorexia nervosa. Consider how stark the situation is when a person whose body is emaciated can look in a mirror and literally see a "fat" body. As much as we have come to know about anorexia nervosa as a disease, it is still one of the most difficult conditions of injurious self-perception to correct. The system of codification is particularly strong, making it untouchable. Unless the code at work in this self-perception can be accessed at the *inter*personal level, there is no possibility for altering the code, and any correction of the injurious self-perception remains impossible.

Finally, consider the case where I believe that the homosexual desire I feel within me is evil and I am being or will be punished for having it. I have resisted recognizing this desire within me, but it remains a barely conscious fact that is subsumed within my system of codification whereby I seek to be a good person who does not perpetuate evil in the world. Unless something outside of me intervenes in a way that allows me to change the way I codify the meaning of my sexual desire so that it is not evil, I will live a life of always having a feeling of evil lurking within and punishment waiting for me. I will work extra hard to present and reinforce all of those things that signify "goodness" as a way of warding off the "evil" that I recognize lurking within me. Moreover, even when I am faced with interventions that provoke my barely conscious awareness of my desire, that allow me to come to consciously reject the notion that homosexual desire is evil, it is still often the case that gay and lesbian people struggle for much of their lives with a deep-seated system of codification in which they are evil or bad for embracing their sexual desire.

THE INTERPERSONAL NETWORK

The second level or network of communication to consider is the interpersonal network. The interpersonal network of communication is radically different from the intrapersonal network. For our present purposes, we shall limit our description of the interpersonal network to communication between two people present in the same time and space. Interpersonal communication entails the potential for equally divided possibilities for receiving, transmitting, and evaluating messages. For people communicating at the interpersonal level, both the origin and destination of messages are known, so feedback can be immediate, and therefore correction of errors is possible. This level of communication holds the greatest capacity for the correction of errors in perception and codification, although the degree to which the correction of errors actually occurs is contingent upon the participants themselves. This is because in our interpersonal communication we will tend toward *either participating or observing.*

As a general principle, we can say that the greater our level of participation, the less our capacity to observe, and vice versa. In other words, in our interpersonal communication there is a basic tendency to be more focused on *experiencing ourselves* or *experiencing the other.* Whichever experience we are tending toward matters because it affects the information we are able to gather, and we will miss information we might have gathered in tending toward the other experience. It is impossible to ever be able to see ourselves perfectly in relation to others. We can never see ourselves as others see us. These conditions constitute "structural constraints" as they are at work at the interpersonal level of communication (Ruesch and Bateson, 1987/1951, p. 79–280).

The interpersonal network or level of communication is the sine qua non of all communication. At this point in our discussion, we are limiting

our description of this network of communication to the situation of two
people communicating with each other in the same time and space. Later,
we shall discover the need to abandon this limit and take up the complexities of this level as they are present in all of the other levels. For now, however, we will develop an example to illustrate the workings of this level of
communication. It will become clear as we work through this example that
things become very complicated very quickly.

The easiest way to illustrate these dynamics of the interpersonal level of
communication is to focus on the process of creating correspondence in
the meaning of the messages as sent and received. You and I are talking.
I hear you say that you and Melinda "had sex." I am startled to hear that
you and Melinda had sex because I thought you were heterosexual, so I say,
"You and Melinda had sex?" Then you repeat yourself, "Melinda and I had
a bet," and now I understand the message correctly. You and Melinda had a
bet. The meaning of your message is made clear to me, and you and I both
know, in part because of my mistake, that we both understand the message
the same way. On a purely informational level we can now proceed in our
conversation knowing that we both understand what we are talking about.

This example illustrates how the potentials for sending and receiving
have made the correction of error possible. I was able to respond immediately by shifting my focus from receiving to sending, and you were able to
respond reciprocally. We then shifted again, and the error in understanding
was corrected. It was obvious that because you and I were talking directly
to each other, we were each asserting our effort primarily toward experiencing the other (observing/receiving) or experiencing ourselves (participat-
ing/sending). When I heard you say that you and Melinda "had sex," the
information carried in that message made me shift from experiencing you
to experiencing me because the message conflicted with what I understood
about you. I made my experiencing of myself present to you by repeating,
"You and Melinda had sex?" You then become aware of how I was experiencing you and you corrected me by repeating, "Melinda and I had a bet."

This example illustrates a very common aspect of everyday communication. We go through this process of sending and receiving, participating
and observing, experiencing ourselves and experiencing the other countless
times every day without thinking. On a purely informational level, these
processes constitute a major part of what we do to get along in our everyday
lives. It is a major way we make sure that we are coordinated with others in
our understanding of what is happening.

As I am sure that you can imagine, however, there is much more going
on in this example than just the exchange and correction of information. At
the level of our participation and observation, the pure information—the
correction of "had sex" to "had a bet"—is neutral. It is simply a fact that
you said one thing and I heard another thing. But the meaning that we

make from this exchange extends, in all likelihood, far beyond the mere correction of information. Both you and I are very aware that the error in my observation is highly suggestive. For me to have heard you say that you and Melinda "had sex" means, in all likelihood, that somewhere in my own thinking I was prepared to hear that you and Melinda did in fact have sex even though I "know" you to be heterosexual. Perhaps at that moment of my startled reaction I recognized for the first time that I did, indeed, think that you might be sexually attracted to women even though I fully accepted your self-presentation as heterosexual. At the same time, upon hearing me convey that I heard you say that you and Melinda "had sex," you became aware that I considered it possible that you in fact did have sex with Melinda. In the immediacy of this exchange you and I both recognize that there could very well be a shift in how each of us sees the other seeing ourself. I recognize that it is possible that you now see me seeing you as potentially sexually attracted to women. You recognize me as seeing you as potentially sexually attracted to women. You might even wonder if I had heard you correctly and at a subconscious level you wish you and Melinda had "had sex," so when you thought you formulated the words "had a bet," you might very well have said, "had sex." Now you ask yourself how it would be if you and Melinda did have sex.

Let's continue with this example and say that after we made this quick correction of information, we each experienced a bit of a startle, but since you were in the middle of telling me a story about you and Melinda, you continued with that story, and neither of us addressed the possible significance of my error. All of the communication that occurred in the immediacy of that exchange does not go away just because on the surface of things we continued on in the conversation about you and Melinda having a bet. It is quite likely that this moment of communication then becomes a *context* that contextualizes our next conversation and perhaps even all of our future communication. You and I have been friends for a while. In our friendship we have established that you are straight and I am not. Melinda is a mutual friend who we both know is sexually interested in both men and women. It is possible for us to simply disregard any possible significance of this "correction of error," and continue within these general presumptions about ourselves and our relationship. I think it is easy to see, however, that it is at least equally likely to remain present as an acknowledged or unacknowledged relational context well into our future.

Let's say that we have never talked explicitly about our respective sexual attractions, and the knowledge that you are straight and I am not has remained comfortably in the background of our friendship for quite a while. Upon this moment of correction of information the entire scope of our communication may change. You may wonder why it is I could think that you and Melinda had sex and if I see something in you that would make me think that you are sexually attracted to Melinda. I may wonder if I in-sulted you, or if you otherwise felt offended or threatened by what I had said. I may be wary of addressing the topic at all and seek to reaffirm my presumption of your heterosexuality in all of my future conversations with you. But, make no mistake about it, even if I make this choice, things do not simply return to how there were before even if we never talk about it again. Maybe I am actually sexually attracted to you, but I am fearful that if I were to be honest with you about that I might lose you as a friend so I am unwilling to address the issue. Or, perhaps I hate the way you flaunt your heterosexuality when you are among us who are not, and I unconsciously want you to feel uncomfortable in how I perceive you.

Similarly for you. You may want desperately to ask me if I do in fact think that you could be sexually attracted to women. But asking that question of me directly is risky. Perhaps you really want me to say, "Yes." Then you take the risk of me saying, "No." Perhaps you were taken aback by what I said and you start questioning why you hang around with people who are not heterosexual. Maybe you decide to distance yourself from me and spend more time around your clearly heterosexual friends. Or, perhaps our differ-ences in sexual attraction are part of what we like about each other, and we have had many playful conversations about you having sex with women. As a result, this "mistake" creates an opening that you then take to talk with me directly about your sexual desire. We could literally go on and on with possible scenarios as to what is going on here.

The interpersonal level of communication illustrates in very clear terms that communication is not and cannot ever be taken to be simply the exchange of information. We must be very careful in our study of our experience of sexuality to recognize the difference between mere information and the fact of communication. Our understanding of "successful communication" must never be reduced to the level of information understood. We shall return to this point throughout our study of our experience of sexuality.

THE GROUP NETWORK

The study of group communication is often dominated by a focus on work-places. We know that when people work in coordination with others within an organization they are subjected to many formal and structural features that largely define their communication activities within the organization. Supervisors can tell supervisees how to behave, what to accomplish, even how to think. Supervisors can dictate many aspects of a supervisee's life within the workplace. Organizational hierarchies are clear examples of formally established structures of communication. We recognize the norms involved in following these formal hierarchies. We also recognize these as "structural constraints" that often provide clearly delimited possibilities for both the exchange of information and the fact of communication.

We also know that the information we get is dependent on our location within the organization and designed to convey what is relevant for us to fulfill our function within the group or organization. We know that others within the organization are privy to different kinds of information. People working in human resources or who are responsible for employee reviews, for example, are bound by specific codes of confidentiality. Many of these restrictions on information and knowledge are in service of a common goal shared by all in the organization, and they serve to make boundaries clear and established. Having clear and established boundaries often supports effectiveness of communication and coordination and can be a sign of very healthy group-level communication. It is also true, however, that in workplaces dominated by gossip, favoritism, and mistrust, these very same "boundaries" can be used in service of individual interests and against the interests of the group. The selective violation of these boundaries, or the withholding or distorting of information, can be used like weapons to damage or limit the success of specific people or subgroups within the organization.

At the purely informational level of communication, the group level is far more complex than the interpersonal level. It is also different from the interpersonal level in that the number of participants can vary widely. In terms of a formal definition, a "small group" is usually defined as three to seven people who share a common goal. There is no clear numerical upper limit on "large groups," but even a very large corporation can share some and perhaps even all of the characteristics of small groups, although the dynamics of group communication obviously become more complex as the size and structure of the group increases. The smaller the group, the more the dynamics resemble what happens at the interpersonal level. The larger the group, the more the dynamics resemble what happens at the intergroup level. This is an important point that will come into play when we move to the discussion of the intergroup level.

In terms of the basic characteristics of the group level or network of communication, the origin and destination of messages is often known, but the larger the group the more likely it is that either the origin or the destination of messages is known, but not both. The correction of messages is possible, but because more channels of communication are involved at this level, correction is often delayed. In larger groups the correction of messages is possible only by shortcutting the established channels of communication. This "shortcutting" begins when the group number exceeds 150. Participants communicate through channels that can separate messages in time and space, which allows for greater distortion. The larger or more complex and differentiated the group, the less complete will be the information available to any given person. Group communication involves a directional flow of messages within the group that will flow either from one to many, or from many to one. These characteristics constitute the "structural constraints" at work at the group level of communication (Ruesch and Bateson, 1987/1951, 280–81).

We will continue with our example of you and Melinda having "a bet" to illustrate what happens in small group communication. Recall that you and I had a miscommunication wherein I thought you said that you and Melinda "had sex." In fact, however, you said that you and Melinda "had a bet." I made you aware of what I heard, and you were then able to correct my error in understanding. As I pointed out above, this moment of "error correction" between you and me is much more than a simple correction at the level of information. Not only do we each speculate as to the "hidden" meanings entailed in our "misunderstanding," but the "misunderstanding" itself reflects on the small group of friends we share. I put "misunderstanding" in quotation marks because we need to be clear that it is a "misunderstanding" at the informational level, but in point of fact this could very well be or become a point of "understanding" revealed at the communicational level.

The group context is important because you and I are friends within a small group of, say, five friends, who have identified among ourselves differences in sexual attractions according to the codes provided by the dominant culture. So, we know that I am a "lesbian," that Melinda is "bisexual," and you are a "heterosexual female." We easily identify the other members of our small group of friends with this cluster of cultural labels. Let's say that the circumstances of our group's friendships have grown out of the fact that we are all communication majors and have had several classes together. At some point we began studying together, and in some classes have been assigned to work with each other on group projects. With this common background, it has become easy for us to exchange information about each other through our group-based lines of communication. When a subgroup of our group gets together, we commonly share information about the other members of the group who are not present. This is not malicious, just our ordinary need to coordinate activities, and a healthy interest in learning about each other. I ask you about Melinda, not to gossip behind her back, but because I know that you had class with her earlier and I wanted to check and see how things were going. The same interests and motivations are at work when you and Melinda talk about me. Because we have readily identified each other using the dominant cultural labels of the day—heterosexual, homosexual, and bisexual—we easily recognize differences among us and those easily become topics of our ongoing conversations.

At this point we can begin to detail the specific characteristics of the small-group level or network of communication. Let's say that after you and I corrected our "misunderstanding" about you and Melinda, we end up talking about how you feel about Melinda, how I feel about you, and how you feel about yourself. At this point you might ask me to keep our conversation confidential because you are not sure what you want the other members of our group to know about your most recent ponderings on these issues. This might be especially important to the degree that we have all fully settled on the adequacy of our labels for each other. If we hold strong presumptions about the adequacy of these labels, then it becomes much more risky for any one of us to think or act in ways that might contradict this shared knowledge we have of each other. We have now established a particular path of communication in which some information is withheld from some members of the group. We all probably know that each of us knows different things about each other, but it is difficult to know how specific or deliberately filtered those "different things" are.

Now, because we are a small group of friends who know each other fairly well and interact regularly, some of us might notice a certain shift in the way you are responding to Melinda. You are probably trying to act like nothing has changed, but of course, something has. The change in the way you relate to Melinda is subtle, and no one can really point to something specific as evidence of this change. But now, Steven, who is a gay man, senses that there seems to be a "message" of some sort going around the group. It is a barely perceivable "message," and even though he recognizes it, he is uncertain of its origin or destination. He makes a mental note to ask you, or another of us, about it at some future point. Thus, there is a delay in our effort to correctly understand what is going on. Steven wonders if, after all, it could all just be a figment of his imagination.

Let's say that Steven thinks about it and decides that he is uncertain if he really even "saw" anything, so he decides to ask me if I saw anything. Or, maybe he decides it is safer to ask Melinda, who as a bisexual may be less "biased." But then it turns out that before Steven gets a chance to talk to anyone, I decided to ask Steven about what he thinks about you and Melinda. Over a period of time all of us are communicating about you, but not directly to you. We come to decide that it is very possible that are sexually are attracted to Melinda because as we have observed you over the intervening time we have noticed a particular energy that you seem to exhibit when Melinda comes around. We have also noticed that Melinda reciprocates this energy, and now we are all saying to ourselves—but not you and Melinda—"Look at them! They might as well take their clothes off and jump into bed right now!" We don't say it directly, but now we begin hinting to each of you that you two should do things together, or spend time together, and so on. You begin to get the message that we think you and Melinda should explore developing a closer relationship, yet the exact origin of this message is unclear. In this scenario, the group function is that of messages being sent from "many to one." As this scenario has developed, it happens that the messages "from the many" are consistent. But imagine how complicated things could become if those messages were contradictory. When the directional flow of messages is from many to one, there is often a limit as to how much information can be fully taken in by the one.

Another possibility is that as you begin to recognize these group-level messages you are receiving, you decide that you need to put a stop to it. You have talked with Melinda and decided that you both share a mutual attraction, but you are not sure what all that attraction entails. You share with Melinda that you think it might just be curiosity and not a real sexual desire. Melinda shares with you her caution about being experimental material for curious straight girls. You both decide to give yourselves time and space to think things through a little bit. Meanwhile, the group's attitude of "wish they'd just go ahead and have sex" remains strong, so you decide that you need to send a very clear message to the group. The next time we are all gathered together you tell us that you recognize that we've been wondering about you and Melinda. You tell us that you've been wondering about you and Melinda, too. You ask us to lay off on the speculation, to stop trying to label you as "bi" or "lesbian," because you just really need some time and space to figure out what your desires really are. You tell us that you consider us your closest friends, and the last thing you want is to alienate any of us. You just want us to ease up on the pressure.

Hopefully, we all understand your message and respect its intent. But, perhaps I am a little disjointed in the way I hear your message because it is true that my initial "error in understanding" occurred because I am, in fact, sexually attracted to you. Reacting from my own insecurities, I feel the desire to disrupt your efforts. I feel a sense of jealously that you are figuring all this out with Melinda, and I may end up acting contrary to your wishes by continuing to put pressure on you hoping to undermine your relationship with her.

We could easily imagine many other scenarios as to how these basic conditions of small-group communication could work out. Regardless of the particulars, however, each scenario would reveal the difficulties that can come with group communication that flows from one to many. No matter how clear and precise the "one" is in communicating with the "many," the "one" can never fully anticipate or control the perspectives or interests through which the "many" will interpret the message.

THE INTERGROUP NETWORK

As we turn now to consider the final level or network of communication, we should recall that each level has been differentiated according to the potentialities of receiving, transmitting, and evaluating messages. We noted that at the group level these potentialities of receiving, transmitting, and evaluating vary according to the size and complexity of the group. In contrast to the other three levels of communication, intergroup network or level of communication involves many people communicating with many people. Neither the origin nor destination of messages can be known, and people are unknowing senders and receivers of messages. Messages are conveyed implicitly in the everyday way people go about their lives and are often remains simply a description of one's everyday way of living (Ruesch and Bateson, 1987/1951, pp. 281–82).

Our institutions function at the level of intergroup communication, often constituting a relationship in which institutions are communicating with institutions. Consider, for example, the codifications of human conduct carried in our legal institutions. These bear obvious connections to religious institutions, as in "one shall not kill." Yet, the codification of "one shall not kill" has exceptions, as in when the state authorizes executions. The codification of "marriage" is, at present, a point of high contention within our culture between our civil and religious institutions. This example illustrates just how powerful the issue of codification is. Many of our most "left-leaning" politicians support the idea of civil unions for gay and lesbian people, but also support the idea that "marriage" remain reserved for male-female relationships.

There is also a time-binding and space-binding aspect to the intergroup level of communication in that the shared codes of communication and practice are passed through from generation to generation as tacit knowledge. We will never be able to fully appreciate the many aspects of our habits of thinking and acting that are directly linked to our ancestors, but they are certainly there. No matter the passage of time or the movement across space, these codes of communication are carried through. Indeed, this is the basic component in the carrying on of a culture.

In contrast to the communication that occurs between large groups like institutions, consider what happens in smaller intergroup communication. Smaller groups have less delay in the correction of messages, and it is easier to detect the origin and destination of messages. We noted that the dynamics of smaller groups tend to resemble the dynamics of interpersonal communication, and that larger groups tend to resemble the dynamics of intergroup communication. We also noted that both the group and interpersonal levels of communication have the capacity for the correction of errors, and this is in part because feedback allows for clarification at the level of code. The *intra*personal level of communication stands in stark contrast to the group and interpersonal levels because at the *intra*personal level the system of codification is impossible to examine and the correction of errors is therefore impossible. In this sense, the intrapersonal level of communication is radically different from the interpersonal and group levels of communication. It is also this difference from the interpersonal and group levels that distinguishes the intergroup level and makes the intergroup level of communication most closely aligned with the *intra*personal level. This is a very important point.

Like the intrapersonal level of communication, the intergroup level of communication functions in ways that are beyond our capacity to examine directly, and therefore the correction of errors is impossible. Consider, for example, the problem of "correcting" errors at the level of culture. In the United States, we "corrected" the problem of slavery, but the issues connected to slavery's most important defining characteristic—black people and not white people are slaves—remains with us in multiple and complex ways. The fact of blackness remains a basic differentiator of human beings within U.S. American culture, and this differentiation retains its capacity for creating a hierarchy of judgment wherein white is better than black. That is not to say that every member of our culture operates according to a logic which tells us that white is good and black is bad, but simply that those significations still circulate easily within the intergroup level of communication and are incapable of being "corrected" because the origin and destination of these messages as they are circulating in the immediacy of our communication with self and others regarding skin color are unknown. Thus, we can sincerely say that we don't judge people based on skin color even while our interactions with others are often based on stereotypes associated with skin color.

The common formulation of this is "I don't see color, I just see a person." First of all, the statement already conveys cultural knowledge that the person speaking it is more than likely white and is referring to people who are not white. The best possible meaning intended with such a message conveys that this person with dark skin with whom I have formed a lasting friendship appears to me as so much more than a skin color. The details we know of each other's lives far surpass any leftovers of stereotypic significations. It is not literally true that we do not see their color.

The "uncorrectable error" occurs when we make this assertion of not seeing skin color as a general claim of perception, especially since the discursive use of the word "color" makes it a marked term even when part of a disclaimer. Thus, to claim that any time I meet or interact with a new person, I do not see the color of his or her skin is simply not accurate unless one is blind. People will vary in the degree to which skin color invokes stereotypical meanings, but it is difficult to believe that we have reached a place where skin color is a minor element in our perception of human beings. While this condition of a "colorless" society is certainly a laudable goal, we have not yet arrived there. To presume we have arrived there is to fail to recognize the ways in which stereotypic significations of skin color remain in circulation and easily available to us. Some of us will have great difficulty recognizing how these stereotypical significations remain at work, while others more easily incorporate perspectives that counter these meanings.

The flip side of this denial of perception is the infamous statement made by Supreme Court Justice Potter Stewart (1964) regarding the definition of obscenity: "I know it when I see it" (Jacobellis v. Ohio, 378 U.S. 184). The certainty we have of *our own* perception, whether in a form of not seeing or seeing, is made possible by the intergroup level or network of communication wherein we have an implicit certainty about our knowledge, yet cannot point to how that knowledge came about.

A final example of intergroup communication for us to consider is the case of adolescent peer groups. This is important because the challenges of adolescence and the power of peer groups at this point in our lives is very significant and can be hugely consequential for our futures. The rise in bullying and recent increase in the incidence of suicide among gay teenagers reflects just how powerful the intergroup level of communication can be at this time in one's life. At some point in the lives of adolescents, they become aware of issues related to sexuality. By the time of adolescence, young people have, of course, been bombarded with messages from media of all sorts about sexuality and sexual relationships—and all of this occurs primarily at the intergroup level. The key about adolescence, which is different from young children "playing doctor," is that their group-level interactions include an expectation that their understanding and behavior should begin to reflect what adults do.

Within adolescent peer groups we often have a distribution of power and influence according to "popularity," or the shared perception as to who most exhibits what the group aspires to. That shared aspiration is usually some version of whatever is "sexy" and "sophisticated," or "rebellious" and "independent." Given the particular community within which this peer group is situated, the exact nature of this shared aspiration within the group will vary. Students at a private high school in a very affluent area defined by the yacht club, the riding stables, summer vacations in Europe, and so on, will have a very different set of aspirations from students at a public school in a working-class neighborhood, for example. Because of their common location in time and space—their shared community—the peer group itself often does not have to negotiate the particulars of what constitutes "popularity." Everyone simply knows who is "popular" and, therefore, sits atop the social hierarchy.

COMMUNICATION THEORY AND INFORMATION THEORY

Our discussion of the four basic levels or networks of communication has been from a perspective that appears to be outside of any one of them.

Our discussion has focused on describing the characteristics or "structural constraints" of communication at each level and on providing examples to illustrate those features and functions. In looking at the subject matter in this way, we have positioned ourselves as neutral observers. Perhaps you believe that you will be tested on this *information* so you presume this information to be static, or unchanging. You take a position as an observer of the information that you think will be exactly what appears to you now on our next examination. You accept the context I have provided in presenting the information, and you know that the testing of your knowledge within that context will be judged according to a binary logic of correct or incorrect. You hope that your mere observation of the information does not change it, or that your interpretation and understanding do not distort the information as it has been presented, and you rely on the interpersonal network as much as you can (by talking to me and your classmates) to create a correct correspondence of meaning. You hope that by focusing carefully at receiving the information accurately you will have the best chance of performing well on the exam. You have, basically, taken an *information theoretic* perspective with regard to the material presented.

Despite the fact that we have sought to position ourselves as neutral observers, we can never achieve this fully. In other words, as human beings we can never really be purely information theoretic in our perception and expression. We often operate on the belief that if we can isolate information outside of any context—therefore presuming that it constitutes its own context to which we are beholden—and achieve a straightforward memorization of it, then we can be assured in the correspondence of meaning between the material presented and our understanding. This is a legitimate way of learning, but it is also limited in cultivating our capacity for perception, and thus also our analytic and critical-thinking skills. It is also limited in cultivating greater self-awareness and self-understanding. Thus, it does not serve us well to approach the study of our experience of sexuality by privileging a process of memorization or replication wherein the particulars and contingencies of experience are excluded. The specific meanings of terms and concepts are important, and may need to be memorized. But their importance lies not in their memorization, but in how that memorization allows us to further our thinking about the subject matter at hand.

It is likely that throughout your reading thus far, the examples offered have generated some self-reflection concerning your own experience as it is both similar to and different from those scenarios described. In other words, the examples have allowed you to select your own context through which to consider and evaluate, not just the information, but your relationship to it. You have *certainty* about your understanding of your own experience in light of the material you have studied. It is the case that the more you were able to select your own context and connect your own experiences to those described, the more certainty you have and the more likely you are to remember them. Once this has happened, the association between your experience and the information contained conveyed in the examples becomes stronger, and you are more likely to retain the information because you have been in *communication* with it. In this way, your reading of the material and its examples generates communication entailing both message and code wherein a *consciousness of experience* emerges. This type of learning is radically different from information-defined learning, and it is a basic requirement for our successful study of our experience of sexuality. Taking account of how it is that this particular conscious awareness becomes present to us is a main—although not the only—task of phenomenological research. Learning to do this kind of human science research requires a specific understanding of the philosophical and practical priorities of phenomenology.

Phenomenology is often understood incorrectly as a variant of qualitative methodologies. When we talk about qualitative methodologies (ethnography, narrative analysis, and so on) we generally understand them to be "methodologically different" from the physical sciences (and their social science derivatives). In other words, qualitative methodologies are distinguished according to the different ways of collecting "data," different ways of managing the "data," and different ways of analyzing the "data," and so on. Within such an approach a researcher can choose among a variety of methods without necessarily having to rethink the epistemological and ontological presuppositions entailed within each because they are basically the same.

To understand phenomenology in this way, as one of a variety of qualitative methodologies that provides different techniques for research, is incorrect. Phenomenology must be understood as "essentially different" from physical science both theoretically and practically (Lanigan, 1988, p. 7). As we move toward our application of semiotic phenomenology as a research procedure, it is important that we understand the "essential difference" between phenomenology and qualitative research methods that work within an information theoretic logic—that is, with *data* exclusively.

It is important to note that Western cultural and "scientific" sense-making privileges metaphysical presumptions that are consistent with the information theoretic perspectives of the physical sciences. Such a perspective *cannot* form or inform the basis for a phenomenological understanding of persons and the world. It is crucially important that we come to see the ways in which our own perception and sense-making are rooted within particular cultural dispositions. Once we do this, it becomes more possible to see this "essential difference" between phenomenology as a human science and qualitative methodologies as social science. It is very important that we become highly attuned to how we are thinking and experiencing as we pursue our study of our experience of sexuality.

The distinction between *information theory* and *communication theory* is especially important in this effort. Information theory (Shannon and Weaver, 1949) is "a mathematical theory designed to measure the amount of information that can be transmitted along a defined channel . . . The term *information* is used in a specialist sense to refer to the predictability of the signal, that is, its physical form, not its meaning" (O'Sullivan et al., 1994, p. 151). Information theory works to reduce uncertainty by exclusion (Lanigan, 1992, p. 211). It is governed by a "digital logic that constitutes *probability* differentiation by exclusion" (p. 211). It functions within a *context of choice*, which means that all probabilities and reductions of uncertainty remain tied to that context of choice. Information theory is formalized as: "{Either [Either/Or] or [Both/And]} (p. 211).

Communication theory, in contrast, entails a "binary analogue logic that constitutes *possibility* differentiation (i.e., certainty) by combination; simply formulated as a 'choice of context'" (Lanigan, 1992, p. 210). Communication theory is formalized as: {Both [Both/And] And [Either/Or]}. Communication theory entails information theory, but not the reverse.

The significance of these differences between information theory and communication theory is difficult to understate. As embodied beings we cannot help but interact with others and our environment in a communication theoretic way—that is, we live comfortably with our own contradictions and paradoxical understanding; we understand our own humor and use of it along with irony and sarcasm. In short, we construct certainty.

The concepts we discussed in the previous chapter all help us understand the basic fact that as embodied human beings we understand nothing except in relationship to something else. This "possibility by combination" occurs at every level of perception and expression. Our ability to understand a spoken word, for example, is based on our ability to recognize combinations and sequences of different sounds (phonemes). Equally, our ability to have a sense of self and world is based on our ability to recognize differences and similarities between our Self and an Other.

Table 5.1. Information Theory versus Communication Theory (Lanigan, 1992, pp. 210–211)

Information Theory	Communication Theory
Digital Logic	Binary Analogue Logic
{Either [Either/Or] or [Both/And]}	{Both [Both/And] And [Either/Or]}
Probability by Differentiation	Possibility by Combination
Reduction of Uncertainty	Construction of Certainty
Context of Choice	Choice of Context

Because we live in a culture that privileges the presumption of a reality that we can come to know as it exists separate from any human being, we do not see the many ways in which the contradictions or inconsistencies we find intolerable in another person's argument or point of view live quite comfortably within our own thinking. The easiest example of this is when parents say to their children, "Do as I say and not as I do." In some cases, like drinking alcohol, we recognize legitimate differences between childhood and adult existence and accept the idea of different standards of behavior for each as noncontradictory. In a case of marital infidelity, however, it may be quite easy for the "cheating" spouse to explain away his or her behavior as more complicated than a teenage child could understand, and that the parent's behavior is really about "protecting" the child by lying to the family.

If, upon considering this example, you form a quick opinion that the "cheating" parent is wrong and is actually hurting the family by lying, then you are demanding that the "cheating" parent be judged according to your information theoretic point of view—that is, an "either/or" logic of an always consistent standard of right and wrong. Contextual factors do not matter because, from your point of view, the marriage vow is sacred, and there is simply no way to justify breaking that vow. To take a communication theory point of view is not to take a relativist stance whereby everything is context-dependent, and we can thereby justify even the most harmful behavior because, say, "he [or she] grew up in an abusive environment." Rather, to take a communication theory point of view is to recognize the difference between the context I select for thinking (marriage vows are sacred and should not, under any circumstances, be violated) and the context within which the person whose behavior I am considering acted. This is the first step of a communication theoretic point of view: recognizing the both/and possibility of self and other. For communication theory to be in full force, however, we must also incorporate the either/or: {Both [Both/And] And [Either/Or]}. Thus, we recognize that in our human relationships, contexts function by selection, and the either/or choices that we easily judge in others as right or wrong, good or bad, always involve our own selection of context.

This is not to suggest that we should always (or even sometimes) refrain from judgment of others' behavior or thinking. Communication theory does, after all, entail information theory. Rather, it is to suggest that the "reality" of what is happening in communication requires us to recognize the importance of context selection in our communication behavior and sense-making. In recognizing this, we actually come closer to the concrete, immediate, and embodied world in which "reality" and our experience of it unfolded. Once we take an information theoretic point of view, however, we fix our own sense of the "reality" of the situation and remain locked within that context, now taken as universal. Upon taking this point of view we terminate our ability to attend to the reality of embodied experience of others and continue on seeing and understanding the world according to us. In short, to think in an information theoretic way excludes the possibility of thinking in a communication theoretic way even though we cannot help but live according to the logic of communication theory.

We shall conclude our discussion of information theory and communication theory by illustrating their function with the exemplars of human speech and gesture. Within the digital logic of information theory "you either speak or you are silent; you either gesture or you remain still. Any choice made provides 'information'—that is, a probability for the next useful choice" (Lanigan, 1988, p. 177). Information theory yields data.

When it comes to the binary analog logic of communication theory, human speech and gesture are again exemplars: "You have both speech and silence when you speak (what is said is concretely contextualized with what is simultaneously not said, but can be said. Also, you have both gesture and its absence (what is done bounds that of which you are capable). Any choice provides a 'message'—that is, a defined context of possibility normative for the choice made" (Lanigan, 1988, p. 177). Communication theory yields *capta*.

In communication theory, the choice *not* made is relevant in that it contextualizes the choice made. As human beings we remember the choice not made and have an awareness of *that which might have been*. You made an either/or decision, but it remains a both/and reality for you because the choice not made can be equally or more relevant than the choice made. The "uniqueness of a binary analogue logic" lies in "the ability to use one logic to code another—for example, coding an analogue logic by a digital logic" (Lanigan, 1988, p. 177). This capacity for using a binary analog logic is what differentiates human from both animal and machine (computer) communication and provides the basis for consciousness. As Lanigan puts it, "Thus, *consciousness* is a referential context that is moved around, fixed, or changed again by mere choice to do so in the coding of the coded system. Yet such consciousness is always bounded by the human agent, the person, who applies the logic of consciousness to consciousness itself thereby creating *experience*" (1988, p. 177).

CONCLUSION

Whatever it is we come to experience is never just a result of our own isolated or autonomous selves moving through the circumstances of life. I have pointed out that because we are social beings we are always situated in the particulars of our historical time, social place, and cultural practices.

The fact that we are always and inextricably located within these particulars of our social and cultural time and place means that any direct examination of our lived-experience of sexuality must move beyond a self-reflection that takes itself to be capable of examining experience as if it lies outside of a position within social and cultural time and space. Our study of our experience of sexuality must examine the very terms and conditions in which it became possible to have had the experience we did.

Our discussion of phenomenology in communicology has emphasized the fact and consequence of our human situatedness in a living world of others. We have discussed the fact of our human contingency as it interrelated within Ruesch and Bateson's (1987/1951) four networks of communication. The discussion illustrates the characteristics and constraints of communication at each of the four levels. Because all four levels are present at all times, it is simply the case that human perception will select the relevant context for our communication behavior. This allows us to illustrate the fundamental difference between information theory and communication theory, and thus also, how the phenomenological emphasis in communicology allows us to move beyond the cultural and "scientific" norms of our Western cultural orientation that would have us ignore or otherwise try to eliminate the very human presence which makes the assertion of all knowledge possible.

FOR FURTHER READING

Hubert G. Alexander, *The Language and Logic of Philosophy* (Lanham, Md.: University Press of America, 1988/1967).

Richard L. Lanigan, "Life-History Interviews: A Teaching and Research Model for Semiotic Phenomenology," In *Phenomenology of Communication: Merleau-Ponty's Thematics in Communicology and Semiology* (Pittsburgh, Pa.: Duquesne University Press, 1988), 144–53.

Ernst Wolfgang Orth, trans. J. N. Mohanty, "Ernst Cassirer," in *Encyclopedia of Phenomenology*, ed. Lester Embree et al. (Boston: Kluwer Academic Publishers, 1997), 95–99.

6

Semiotic Phenomenology

Semiotic phenomenology is the methodological foundation of communicology. The conjunction of the two terms "semiotic" and "phenomenology" stakes out both a philosophical orientation and a logic of embodiment that establishes the fact and presence of human consciousness as it is situated within the concrete reality of other human consciousnesses and a physical environment. Through nearly four decades of work, Richard Lanigan (1972, 1977, 1984, 1988, 1992) has detailed the precise intellectual developments in Western thought from the classical period to the present through which communicology and semiotic phenomenology have come to be identified as both a philosophy of communication and a human science.

Semiotic phenomenology is, by definition, transdisciplinary. Historically, semiotics has been a featured part of major developments in linguistics, anthropology, and philosophy. The focus on semiotics within linguistics has contributed to the interdisciplinary work roughly called "linguistic psychology." Anthropology, particularly the structuralist anthropology of Claude Lévi-Strauss (1969) and cultural anthropology generally, have made generous use of semiotics and semiotic theory. Linguistic anthropology and sociolinguistics also share significant aspects of their intellectual trajectories with semiotics. The study of discourse, popular culture, and issues related to power, agency, and the legitimizations of knowledge have all used semiotics and semiotic theory to the extent that they problematize the presumed neutrality of rationality and representation as basic to human progress.

Much like semiotics, phenomenology has a history of bringing together different trajectories of thought into ways of thinking and understanding that might not otherwise have developed as such. Most notably in this regard is the bringing together of mathematics, logic, psychology, and

philosophy. Edmund Husserl, considered the founder of phenomenology, was a mathematician whose engagement in the late nineteenth and
early twentieth century debates concerning the adequacy of the physical or
natural sciences as a basis for the study of human beings launched what is
known today as the "phenomenological movement" (Spiegelberg, 1984).
The work of Charles Sanders Peirce, also a mathematician, but with particular accomplishments in logic, featured a clearly phenomenological emphasis in what is typically recognized as semiotic in nature. As we continue with
a communicological approach to the study of our experience of sexuality,
it is important that we are aware that our theoretical and methodological
orientation is rooted in a long and specific history of intellectual work.

My decision to teach communicative sexualities with an applied focus on
the students' lived-experience means that I prioritize the *practice* of semiotic
phenomenology within the thinking, feeling, and speaking that becomes
available to all of us in the classroom as we talk about, listen to, and reflect
on our experience. At the graduate level, it is crucial that this practical focus not substitute for a direct and sustained study of the specific scholarly
trajectories through which communicology and semiotic phenomenology
have been developed. We should bear in mind that the demands of semiotic phenomenology as a research methodology require an advanced study
of these theoretical contributions toward the establishment of communicology. It is far too often the case that qualitative research methodologies
simply take up and reproduce a positivist paradigm in which the research
practice itself is reduced to mere technique or method wherein the method
is "assumed to be its own theoretical explanation" (Lanigan, 1992, p. 18).

My purpose in the present chapter is to lay out the theoretical and methodological foundations of semiotic phenomenology as an applied research
procedure. The theoretical aspect of this discussion is necessary in order
for us to understand the particular subject matter taken up in semiotic
phenomenology—that is, lived-experience. This means that we must understand semiotic phenomenology's particular approach to the human being
as both a particular person and as interconnected with other people within
the structures and signifying systems we have discussed in the previous
chapters. In short, we are interested in the *conjunction of person and culture.*

THE CONJUNCTION OF CULTURE AND PERSON

Once we bring semiotics into relation with phenomenology, our focus
turns from the study of signs and sign-systems to the study of *semiosis,* or
the ongoing action of signs. Sign-systems function at the level of culture
and retain a great deal of consistency across generations of human communities. Language is the most complex of all human sign-systems. As

such, language has often been the privileged object of study within some branches of semiotic theory—an effort we could rightly call an "objective science of language" (Merleau-Ponty, 1964, p. 86). It is also true, however, that the only way humans can know or study language as a sign-system is by using it, by taking it up as both an object and means of study—thus the bringing together of semiotics and phenomenology. The moment we recognize this, we also realize that language itself, as a formal and objectively delineable system, cannot come to be known except in conjunction with the speech of embodied human beings. It is not enough to take up the scientific or observational stance in which we "see language in the past" (p. 84). Human language is much more than an "object before thought" (p. 84). It is, rather, an "an original way of intending certain objects, as thought's body" (p. 84). An examination of semiosis, as opposed to the mere fact of signs and sign-systems, moves us more firmly into a semiotic phenomenology wherein we can engage the dynamic interrelation of speech and body that is human embodiment.

Our own speech and speaking is one of the most intimate and consequential facts of our living-experience. Consider cases of imposed silences related to sexual violation. The fact that silence is imposed—whether explicitly by threat or implicitly, by the deeply felt shame that often comes with sexual violation—has deeply powerful consequences that can and will remain forever present and variously debilitating within the psyche of the person who has been sexually traumatized. For persons who have been sexually traumatized and forced into silence, the ability to come to speak about it in some way or another it is the only means through which the damage of the trauma can be genuinely healed.

Consider also that forbidding persons of a particular cultural group to express themselves in the style and modality of their mother tongue is one of the most effective ways to perpetuate cultural genocide. For bilingual people generally, and children who speak one language at home and another in pubic more specifically, the home language often retains intimacy and closeness that the public language may never come to engender (Rodriguez, 1982). Imagine the consequences for children who grow up in circumstances where the intimacy of the language spoken at home is characterized by derision, ridicule, and threats to safety. Our own language and ability to speak is one of the most intimate and consequential facts of our living-experience.

To take a more benign example—and one more likely to guide us in our application of semiotic phenomenology—consider the experience of being in a relationship and sensing something important about what just happened in the relationship, but not being able to put it into words. In this case, my sense of this important thing is present like a subtle prick in my side. It is there, but it does not really grab my full attention. I do not know the cause of the prick, and other things in my thinking and my surroundings easily take my attention away from this subtle sensation. Later, I am talking with a different friend about this relationship. As I listen to my friend and hear my own speech, I begin to sense again this subtle prick in my side that I sensed earlier. I continue to listen to my friend speak; and as I hear myself speak in response, a new understanding emerges before me, and I come realize that I now see and can articulate what it was that I could only sense previously. I hear myself speak and realize that what I just said is what I have been sensing for a long time. It is in this sense that we say, along with Merleau-Ponty, that speech "accomplishes" thought (1962, p. 178).

Throughout this work I have used the word "culture" in the ordinary sense in which we all understand it. Without formulating a specific definition, our ordinary understanding of the word "culture" is adequate enough so that we are able to understand its use and meaning without much conscious attention. Generally speaking, we understand culture as consisting of patterns of practice, understanding, and preference that are shared and transmitted from generation to generation. The technical part that we must add to this generally sufficient definition is that *culture is re-created through communicative practice*. This is important because too often we understand culture as something that is *given*. Although it is true that we cannot simply chose which parts or aspects of a culture will come to live within us, or how our participation in our cultural norms will sustain and/or change those norms, it is also true that in our actual communicative practices we do, indeed, re-create without ever exactly replicating the cultural norms of the communities and groups within which we live. Because culture is deeply enduring and slow to change, it is difficult, maybe even impossible, to consciously choose how one's behavior or practice will change cultural norms. That does not mean, however, that change is not taking place. When we talk about culture, it is very important that we see it as an orientation toward *preference* that is within each of us and which we actively take up and re-create both preconsciously and unconsciously as a choice of context.

Looking at culture in this contextual way leads us to the notion of *embodiment*. To talk about embodiment allows us to be more precise regarding the relationship between our own personal selves and the culture within which we live. When we talk about embodiment we are referring to the human condition of living within culture whereby humans unconsciously and preconsciously take up and re-create the norms of culture *in experience*. These last two words, "in experience," are crucial. What we experience does not emerge in a vacuum. It is precisely "in experience" that we embody the practices and norms of our culture and community. There is a double-edged sword to this fact that we embody the practices and norms of our culture "in experience." On the one hand, if our experience comprises more than just the idiosyncrasies of our particular selves, then we have access to and can study those aspects of culture that we share with others. On the other hand, because we embody culture it can exist and function completely beneath our conscious awareness, for example, your preconscious practice of wearing clothes in public.

Thus, we turn to the problem of *perception*. Perception is never just a physical or natural capacity of human beings. Neither is it a neutral capacity capable of reconstituting what is perceived separately from the fact of the particular person perceiving—or what we might call the *perceiving subject*. Once we take the perceiving subject seriously, we recognize that our perception and expression are *reversible*. This means that what we come to perceive in our embodied relation to others and the world is always already an *expression* of our interconnection with others and the world (e.g., your choice of *which clothes* to wear in public). Moreover, the particularities of what we express in our communicative behavior are not possible except for the fact that we *perceive* ourselves, others, and the world. This is what it means, in part, to say that communicology "uses the methodology of *semiotic phenomenology* in which the expressive body discloses cultural codes, and cultural codes shape the perceptive body—an ongoing, dialectical, complex helix of twists and turns constituting the reflectivity, reversibility, and reflexivity of consciousness and experience" (Lanigan, 2008, p. 104). We must not take the fact of perception for granted or otherwise fall into the trap of thinking that perception is or can be "pure" or unaffected by social and cultural forces.

When we talk about sexuality, we are most certainly talking about desire. Desire must be understood within this dynamic conjunction of person and culture. There is no doubt that I can recognize sexual desire within my own body and feeling, and that at some points in time this experience of my desire appears wholly my own and separate from any particular object of desire present in the world around me. On the other hand, our understanding of this complex interrelation between person and culture means that desire is never separate from the circumstances in which it emerges. We must understand sexual desire as both social and personal phenomenon, as both conscious and preconscious. We must understand desire as it bears a strong connection to power as socially expressed.

It is crucially important that in our implementation of semiotic phenomenology as a research procedure we not forget or underestimate the importance of this conjunction between person—ourselves as embodied in lived-experience—and culture. Cultural norms and structures will not become expressed in the lived-experience of every person in the same way. Yet, we must be able to see beyond our initial ways of seeing so that we can investigate this very conjunction of ourselves and the world in which we live.

THE RECURSIVE AND SYNERGISTIC THREE-STEP
PROCEDURE OF SEMIOTIC PHENOMENOLOGY

All research involves a systematic process through which we seek to ascertain the accuracy and adequacy of our assertions about what is real and true. Semiotic phenomenology involves a three-part process of phenomenological description, phenomenological reduction, and phenomenological interpretation. This basic three-step process is both *recursive* and *synergistic*. In a theoretical sense, this three-step process is recursive in the sense that each step entails all the other steps (see figure 6.1). Thus, phenomenological description entails description, reduction, and interpretation; phenomenological reduction entails description, reduction, and interpretation, and so on. In short, the moment we try to describe an experience, we have already interpreted it. There is no such thing as a "pure" description of experience.

The implications of this theoretical recursivity for our application of research methodology is that each step within the basic three-step procedure now requires an explicit account of the meaningfulness of the experience—that is, an account of how we thematized the experience in the very imme-

THEORY	METHODOLOGY
Phenomenological Description	
1. DESCRIPTION (entails): a. Description; b. Reduction; c. Interpretation.	1. DESCRIPTION: (Thematizing the) 2. Interpretation (of the) 3. Reduction (of the) 4. Description (of the SIGN).
Phenomenological Reduction	
2. REDUCTION (entails): a. Description; b. Reduction; c. Interpretation.	5. REDUCTION: (Abstracting the) 6. Interpretation (of the) 7. Reduction (of the) 8. Description (of the SIGNIFIER).
Phenomenological Interpretation	
3. INTERPRETATION (entails): a. Description; b. Reduction; c. Interpretation.	9. INTERPRETATION: (Explicating the) 10. Interpretation (of the) 11. Reduction (of the) 12. Description (of the SIGNIFIED).

Figure 6.1.   Theory and Methodology of Semiotic Phenomenology

Source: "Theory and Methodology of Semiotic Phenomenology," from Richard L. Lanigan, *Phenomenology of Communication* (1988), p. 9. Reprinted by permission of Duquesne University Press.

diacy of our experiencing. Recognizing that experience becomes meaning-ful to us only and precisely because we are thematizing it in its immediacy allows us then to backtrack and seek out the "modality" of thematization that led us to experience that experience as we did. Going through this pro-cess allows us to achieve what, in phenomenological terms, we call *invocation of the epochē*, or "bracketing." As a result of these two steps, we can now move to the third step and provide a *description* of our lived-experience.

When we move to the second basic step of semiotic phenomenological research, the *reduction* phase, we engage a process of *abstraction*. We select parts from within the description, or descriptions, and shift them around here and there seeking to make differentiations through our varying com-binations. In phenomenological terms, we call this *imaginative free variation* (IFV). Again, we recognize that our first movements using imaginative free variation entail or are informed by our own interpretation. Although we have invoked the epochē in the first basic step of the research procedure, we must recognize that as we move through each step we are still relying on our already thematized (interpreted) understanding of our experience and the phenomenon. Thus, as we move to the reduction phase where we are abstracting various parts of the description(s) and seeking points of convergence and divergence, we are still mindful of our own imposition of meaning and therefore continue to make that imposition a formal point of examination within the research procedure.

The third basic step of semiotic phenomenological methodology is the interpretation phase. At this point in the research procedure, we begin ex-plicating the essential features of the phenomenon under study. Again, we recognize that our own thematizations or interpretive schemes are at work, and therefore begin this step in the procedure by explicating the interpreta-tion that has generated the description abstracted in the second basic step of the research procedure—that is, the reduction phase. We then continue using imaginative free variation in an effort to fully explicate the phenom-enon under study until we can demonstrate the place and function of the "essential features" that made it possible for the phenomenon under study to emerge in experience as it did.

METHODOLOGICAL SYNERGISM

If the previous discussion leaves you with the feeling that these "three basic steps" in phenomenological research are very complex, deeply intercon-nected, and not entirely distinct, then you are understanding correctly. But, the fact that these three basic steps are complex, interconnected, and not entirely distinct *does not* equate to things being confused. Rather, it merely indicates the proper complexity of our general research effort. Human com-munication, like human experience, is incomprehensibly complex. In all our

efforts to study it, we inevitably make it static or partial. Semiotic phenomenological research is specifically designed to study human communication
holistically and in its dynamic process of happening. This is why the methodological procedures themselves are *synergistic*—and thus require a sophisticated and well-developed ability to see, sense, feel, and describe what is happening at every point in the research procedure. The specialized terminology
of phenomenology provides us with particular *guideposts* or markers that help
us keep clear about where we are in the research procedure.

It is very important that at every stage of the research—particularly when
we get to the point of writing it up for presentation to an interested audience—we need to be able to clearly identify what is happening in which
stage of the research process. This is like making the skeleton visible so that
readers can see how we have attached this to that to get the other. But, on
the flip side of this effort, we want to remember that a completely "clean"
or "accurate" representation of these three steps is never possible precisely
because of the recursivity and synergism of the methodology.

I like to explain the synergism of phenomenological methodology as a
process similar to putting together a jigsaw puzzle. There is no set way for
putting together a jigsaw puzzle except for trial and error—we try this piece,
we try that piece. We look for edges, for hints of color, for the contour of
pieces, we compare to the completed image, and we keep trying until we
get the fit. And when it fits, we *know* it. It is the same process with phenomenological research, except that you must decide on the image and you
must create and contour the pieces as they fit together to make the whole.
For example, culture tells you that there are only four corners (information theory; data = what is given; context of choice), but your embodiment
focuses on particular images that guide the selection and combination of
pieces (communication theory; capta = what is taken; choice of context).
To verify this process, just try to work on a jigsaw puzzle in a small group
of five people where you are instructed *not* to talk. You will see gestures of
five people trying to work on five images!

This analogy of putting together a jigsaw puzzle in which you must decide
the contours, colors, and ultimately the image displayed is important because
it helps us understand a very, very important aspect of doing semiotic phenomenological research: the difference between the order of experience (OE)
and the order of analysis (OA). In recognizing the difference between the
order of analysis and order of experience, we will be able to keep better track
of our application of semiotic phenomenological methodology.

Order of Experience and Order of Analysis

Everything we do in our research is irrevocably tied to the fact that *we
are doing it.* In other words, we must recognize the fact that we are actually
doing something in order to study what was done—we must be able to

take into account the fact that we are present in the research itself. We will take up this issue more directly in chapter 8. For now, however, we need to understand the difference between the *order of experience* (OE) and the *order of analysis* (OA). See figure 6.2 below.

In our ordinary everyday life, we do not typically distinguish what is happening in the order of our experiencing and what we do in any effort to analyze our experience. Notice in figure 6.2 that in every case experience occurs in three basic modalities: an *experiencer, experiencing,* and that which was *experienced.* Traditional social science research retains the basic presumptions of positivism which includes the notion that reality can be known separately and independently from the human being who is observing and experiencing. As a result, there is no need to distinguish between the order of experience and the order of analysis because the experience of doing the research is sought to be made irrelevant in the formal research procedure. For the positivist, who does not recognize the difference between the order of experience and the order of analysis, the things that are studied are simply *given,* as *data,* which must then be analyzed without explicit regard to the

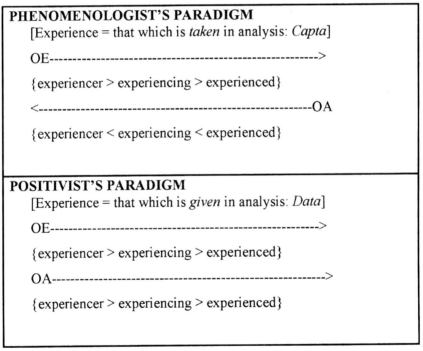

Figure 6.2. Lanigan's Comparative Research Procedure Involving the Order of Experience (OE) and the Order of Analysis (OA)

Source: "Comparative Research Procedure Involving the Order of Experience (OE) and the Order of Analysis (OA)," from Richard L. Lanigan, *The Human Science of Communicology* (1992), p. 20; "Communication Theory" and "Information Theory," Lanigan, *The Human Science of Communicology*, Appendix B, pp. 210–11. Reprinted by permission of Duquesne University Press.

fact of the immediacy and significance of their own human presence in the research practice itself. As Lanigan (1992, p. 18) puts it, because positivists assume the "scientific method" to "be its own theoretical explanation," the order of experience and the order of analysis are made identical, and this "allows the so-called 'objective' condition where the researcher is assumed not to be present, not to be an influence on the research act."

We cannot not take the positivist's approach in our study of communicative sexualities because everything we do and come to see in our research is imminently connected to the fact of our own perception and expression. Instead, we take the phenomenologist's approach in that we recognize that we cannot in any given moment of our human existence take in and make fully transparent to ourselves all that we are perceiving and processing at the unconscious, preconscious, and conscious levels. We understand experience, therefore, as that which is *taken* in analysis—that is, *capta*. We recognize our own process of selection and then hold ourselves accountable to it. We reverse the order of experience in our analyses and begin with that which was experienced because we recognize that what we experienced was itself selected, or taken, from within a very large set of possibilities. As Lanigan (1992, p. 19) summarizes: the phenomenological approach allows us to make three strictly methodological or procedural statements: "These criteria state the semiotic code (communicative message) conditions for the phenomenology of the situation as lived by a person. The phenomenology quite literally becomes the logic of a governing phenomena found in the meaning of the situation under study. Meaning, the signs composed of signifiers and signifieds, constitute the subject/object matter under analysis."

A WALK-THROUGH OF
SEMIOTIC PHENOMENOLOGY APPLIED

Following the work of Ihde (1997) and Van Manen (1990), we can shorthand the three steps of semiotic phenomenology according to the three steps below. New terms are introduced in this shorthand account, and these will be discussed as we move through each step of the walk-through.

1. *Phenomenological Description*: Thematize; invoke the epoché; identify the noema; descriptions of experience as experienced without explanation or reflection;
2. *Phenomenological Reduction*: Abstract; involves the use of imaginative free variation; identify the noesis;
3. *Phenomenological Interpretation*: Explicate the essential structures of the phenomena; specify the correlation of the noesis and noema; discover phenomenological intentionality.

Phenomenological Descriptions

At first glance, the effort to describe one's lived-experience seems obvious and easy. Once we begin this effort, however, we find that it is neither. Part of the reason for this is the fact that "lived experience first of all has a temporal structure; it can never be grasped in its immediate manifestation but only reflectively as past presence" (Van Manen, 1990, p. 36). Try it. Take just five minutes and describe your experience. Okay, what have you described? Was what you described actually what you originally selected to describe? What was "it" that you selected to describe? How close did your description get to "it"? It's a bit of a predicament.

Given this predicament, we will follow the four "operational rules" or "hermeneutical rules" set out by Ihde (1997): First, "attend to the phenomena of experience as they appear" (p. 34); second, *"Describe, don't explain. . . . To describe* phenomena phenomenologically, rather than *explain* them, amounts to selecting a domain for inclusion and a domain for exclusion" (p. 34); "one must carefully delimit the field of experience in such a way that the focus is on describable experience *as* it shows itself" (p. 35); third, *"horizontalize or equalize all immediate phenomena.* Negatively put, do not assume an initial hierarchy of 'realities'" (p. 36); and fourth, *"seek out structural or invariant features of the phenomena"* (p. 39).

The difference between this shorthand version and the full semiotic phenomenological version discussed above is simply that the latter offers a much finer account of what actually happens at each stage of the research procedure. The advantage of Ihde and Van Manen's approach is that they allow us to more easily detect the more obvious sets of ready-made thematizations as provided by our cultural and social groups. These accounts are all entirely theoretically consistent with each other. Lanigan's specification, however, is more theoretically developed and incorporates the full force of Merleau-Ponty's distinction between *speech-speaking* and *speech-spoken* (1981/1945, p. 178). We have not, in the present work, addressed this level of theoretical and practical distinction. We use Ihde and Van Manen because their work is written as an introduction to doing phenomenological research. We are, of course, working at an introductory level.

Notice how rules 1–3 require an invocation of the epochē or "bracketing." To invoke the epochē is to consciously identify our presuppositions at work in our identification and description of the phenomenon under study. In invoking the epochē we do not try to eliminate or forget the fact of our presuppositions. Rather, it is crucial that we simply set them aside—bracket them—for what they allow us to see. In other words, our presuppositions, once identified, provide an important element for differentiation by combination. Because we can see our presuppositions, we can see the phenomenon separately from those presuppositions. We invoke the epochē so that we can get as close as possible to the experience as we

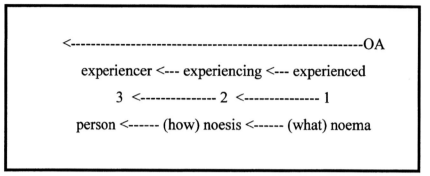

Figure 6.3. Ihde's Phenomenological Process

experienced it without seeing it through our taken-for-granted presumptions or post-hoc rationalizations.

Our understanding relies on the difference between the order of experience (OE) and order of analysis (OA) as discussed above (see figure 6.2). What we take for granted as simply "experience" in fact comes to us already having a structure that entails three dimensions: experiencer—experiencing—experienced. Figure 6.3 above presents Ihde's rendition of Lanigan's figure 6.2. I include Ihde's here because it introduces the language of *noesis* and *noema*.

In phenomenological research, we begin with the "noema," or the "what" that was experienced. Next, we move to the "noesis," or the "how" of experiencing or the "how" or "modality" of experience. Only lastly can we get at the "person" in the experience. I put "person" in quotation marks to emphasize the fact that no person is ever separable from the fact of being located within and inextricable, intersubjectively linked with the semiotic systems of culture and group.

A major problem for people new to phenomenological research is not quite being able to get themselves (the experiencer) or their interviewees (also the experiencer) out of the dominant position within the research. This is why it is important that phenomenological research is never just psychological—that is, it is never really concerned with *why* a particular person feels, says, or does a particular thing; we are *not* interested is psychologizing the person in a way that locates the emergence of experience from strictly within a person. Rather, phenomenological research is interested in the possibilities for experience (and its meaningfulness) across cultural groups as they become actualized in particular instances and thus manifest as typicifications or tendendicies (habits) that are characteristic of a cultural time and place. Phenomenological descriptions must be as faithful as possible to the fact of experiencing. Understanding the difference between noema, the "what" of experience, and noesis, the "how" of experience, allows us to be more faithful to the fact of experiencing and less beholden by our taken-for-granted assumptions about what is real. Ihde's four operational rules identified above also assist in this effort.

Phenomenological Reductions

To understand phenomenological reductions it is important to recall what I wrote above to begin the discussion of phenomenological descriptions: At first glance, the effort to describe one's lived-experience seems obvious and easy. Once we begin this effort, we find that it is neither. Part of the reason for this is the fact that "lived experience first of all has a temporal structure; it can never be grasped in its immediate manifestation but only reflectively as past presence" (Van Manen, 1990, p. 36).

This makes one wonder: Is it ever possible to get a "pure" description? Aren't we always already, inevitably, and despite our best efforts, locked into a "reduction" mode whereby what we come to experience is a result of thematization—in other words, no matter what "phenomena" we experience, we experience them through an already existing frame of meaningfulness? The answer to the former question is, basically, "no, it is not possible to get 'pure' descriptions of experience." And, the answer to the latter question is, basically, "yes, everything we experience comes through an already existing framework of meaningfulness." Herein lies a certain insight to phenomenological theory and practice. We do not delude ourselves about the possibility of getting at a pure description of lived-experience. But, what happens in our nondeluded effort to get at this unattainable pure description of lived-experience is that we uncover those very "always already" present thematizations and make particular experiences possible. Charles Peirce called this logic an *abduction* (Lanigan, 1992, p. 221). In other words, it allows us to account for our experience of *this* or *that* coming into existence. Whatever *this* or *that* is, it never exists separately from our experiencing of it—it is never merely an object in our environment.

The phenomenological reduction is the key to all of phenomenological research. The other two basic steps are essential—we can't do without them. But, the reduction has a special place, both theoretically and practically. Although we talk about beginning the research with description, our previous discussion has already demonstrated that the reduction and interpretation are always there at the start as well.

Well, then, you might ask, what *is* a phenomenological reduction in *practice*? In practice the phenomenological reduction relies on two crucially important movements in thinking. The first we have already discussed above, and that is Imaginative Free Variation (IFV). IFV allows us to shift aspects of our descriptions by focusing on the noesis (modality of experiencing), or noetic context, within which the noema (the what of our experience) emerges. As Ihde (1997, p. 40) puts it, "the use of variations requires obtaining as many *sufficient* examples or variations upon examples as might be necessary to discover the structure features being sought."

The second crucially important movement in thinking during the phenomenological reduction is the attentiveness toward the emergence of "revelatory phrases." It is far too common in qualitative research to presume that a detailed attention to the content (what is given, data) is what brings us to discovery in the research process. This is simply not the case. That is because no matter how attentive we are to the content of experience, we are still separate from it and seeing it through our own perceptual and expressive capacities. Imaginative free variation is a practice that requires our intervention into the data, or the noema of experience. As we do this, we see different aspects of the experience and phenomenon. At particular moments in the reduction phase-aspects of the description(s) will come to strike us in a particular way and we will be ale to identify a specific revelatory phrase through which we can then specify the noetic context which enabled the noema to be experienced as it was. The discovery of "revelatory phrases" moves our research from seeing the varied possibilities of what we think is a phenomenon to discovering the "invariants" that in fact made it possible for the experience to have become experienced as it was. As Ihde puts it, "Variations 'possibilize' phenomena [and] thus are devices that seek the invariants in variants and also seek to determine the limits of a phenomenon" (p. 40).

Phenomenological Interpretations

In colloquial terms, we understand this stage of phenomenological research as the "results"—which is, in fact, what it is. Yet, when we understand the phenomenological interpretation exclusively in terms of the "results" of our research, we tend to concretize the "knowledge" produced through phenomenological research and add it to the stack of "knowledge" we like to measure as contributions. This is *not* the best way to think about the phenomenological interpretation. And the reason is that in thinking this way we tend to presume that knowledge can and should reach a status of "apodictic" certainty (Ihde, 1997, p. 73). Yet, given the concerns and goals of phenomenological research, we realize that such apodictic certainty is not attainable, not desirable, and is a fundamental distortion of the phenomena we study. Thus, we need to think in terms of "adequate" certainty (Ihde, 1997, p. 73). In chapter 7, on "Horizons: Adequacy and Invariance," Ihde offers us a way of understanding the "product" of phenomenological research that is itself reflective of the nature of the phenomena we study.

The aim of the phenomenological interpretation is to discover the essential or invariant structures of a phenomenon which make it possible for it to have appeared (and become experienced by a person) in the way that it did. This is an effort to get at *phenomenological intentionality* (which is not to be confused with our common understanding of "intention" as conscious choice). Phenomenological intentionality (consciousness) is what unites the particular human being to the culture, language, institutions, and other suprasocial semiotic structures (experience) in which we are all inextricably interconnected. The complexity of this inextricably interconnectedness is what accounts for my caution in thinking of this final stage of phenomenological research as a "result" to be added to the "knowledge" we build up and store for future distribution. Yes, we can understand this complexity much more through our phenomenological studies, but we are always, at best, reaching for something that is in part and invariably out of our reach. What we get in that reaching is *meaning* that is valuable as the accumulated *understanding* we call "culture."

We understand that experience comes to us already *structured*; this structure (culture) does *not* determine what our experience is or will be but both constrains and enables it. The suprapersonal semiotic structures of our cultural and social world generate a certain momentum or "tendency toward" (what Peirce calls "capacity") which then gets taken up in correlation with a particular person present in a specific time and place. This correlation reveals how intentionality is at work as an essential or invariant structure of the phenomenon. Because we are dealing with abstractions, when we get to the interpretation phase of the research, it is very important that we return to the specific, concrete, and immediate experience (experiencing) as possible. In other words, we want to discover the *reflexive* condition in which this particular experiencing became what it became.

This reflexive condition is one way of talking about "*phenomenological intentionality*," or the directedness of consciousness. Consciousness is directed by virtue of two brute facts: that we have a body, and that we exist within culture (social structures). That we have a body and exist within culture accounts for the *modalities* in which we live in the world. In phenomenological terms, these modalities provide *noetic contexts*. Within these noetic contexts, specific "things" appear in experience. These "things" that appear constitute the content, or the "what" of our experience. In phenomenological terms, this "what" of our experience is called the *noema*, or *noematic content*. In discovering the correlation between the noesis and the noema we will have discovered phenomenological intentionality, or the reflexive condition in which a particular experience became what it became.

The major difficulty with this effort is the fact that the only way we can attempt to discover intentionality is through *language and reflection*, which necessarily alter the experience itself. Because we cannot avoid this problem, we must be very sensitive to it. We must scrutinize our use of language and be doggedly faithful to the experiencing of the experience. We can never escape the fact that we are *experiencers experiencing the experienced* in an inseparable whole. So, we must interrogate this to the greatest degree possible.

CONCLUSION

My effort in this chapter has been to provide a detailed discussion of semiotic phenomenology as an applied research procedure. I have featured those aspects that most directly inform its application. I have emphasized the significance of human speech as an essential point in the convergence between person and culture. This convergence highlights the need for a methodology that is both recursive and synergistic. A discussion of the relationship between semiotic phenomenological theory and semiotic phenomenological methodology demonstrates how these recursive and synergistic aspects inform the research practice. I detailed the basic research steps of phenomenological description, phenomenological reduction, and phenomenological interpretation, and I addressed the very important distinction between the "order of analysis" and the "order of experience."

Semiotic phenomenology is an applied research methodology. As such, it cannot be reduced to mere technique or procedure. This is because the procedures themselves require a human presence. This means that we must take account of what we actually do in our *practice* of semiotic phenomenology, and all of the variations in thinking, understanding, and experiencing entailed therein. Semiotic phenomenology is a very demanding methodology that requires an advanced understanding of the theoretical and philosophical developments from which it has developed as an applied logic in the human sciences.

FOR FURTHER READING

Calvin O. Schrag, *Communicative Praxis and the Space of Subjectivity* (Bloomington: Indiana University Press, 1986).

Jacqueline M. Martinez, "Racisms, Heterosexisms, Identities: A Semiotic Phenomenology of Self Understanding," *Journal of Homosexuality*, vol. 45, no. 2/3 (1993): 109–27.

J. N. Mohanty, "Meaning," in *Encyclopedia of Phenomenology*, ed. Lester Embree et al. (Boston: Kluwer Academic Publishers, 1997), 443–46.

7

Semiotic Phenomenology Applied

What is your experience of sexuality? With this simple question we set in motion a series of reflections that open the possibility for the discovery of our human presence in the *flesh*. There is no doubt about it: To experience sexuality is to experience fleshiness. We feel sexual arousal within our body, the increased flow of blood throughout, the focusing of internal energies and external attention, the reaching toward the other's body with one's own peaked sensitivities of fingertips, hands, lips, mouth, tongue, nipples, genitals, pressing movement from within one's own body extending toward the other, seeking contact, immersions in moisture heated with growing electricity, insatiable desire moving of its own accord, no longer identifiable with a specific location or body part but fused in a totality of fleshy bodies reverberating in and through each other.

To experience the fleshiness of sexuality in this way, as a totality of one's body moving in energetically driven accordance with another, is not an inevitable or determined outcome of having or recognizing one's sexual desire. It is, rather, an achievement contingent upon a vast array of circumstances, dispositions, and behaviors that can vary greatly from person to person and moment to moment. I think we all know that just because we can recognize in our bodies the fleshiness of sexual desire happily fulfilled does not mean that we can or will be able to create the circumstances in which such desires can be realized just because we want them to be. What we know to be our own sense of sexual desire and fulfillment does not typically become realized in our body as if flipping a switch—such a realization requires an entire situation in which things can come to unfold in a certain accordance. The specific terms and conditions of this accordance wherein a total experience of our flesh with another's becomes realized can vary greatly. In some sets of circumstances and actions it can be that the situation is relatively clear and straightforward, while in others the situation can be highly confused and convoluted. It is also true that the interrelation within our own body, between our thinking and feeling, can be relatively clear and straightforward or highly confused and convoluted. My body feels, but my mind holds my feelings at bay. My mind sees and thinks how good it could feel, but my body is distant and not responding in the way my mind hopes. Every body is unique, and all bodies change over time, and therefore the relative level or degree of desire for intensely sexual experiences varies both from person to person and within the life span of people generally.

Thus, it is important that we begin our application of semiotic phenomenology by invoking the phenomenological epochē and recognize that sex is never really ever just sex. Sexuality can, in theory, be a case of a mechanical body seeking fulfillment—like when I have an itch on my back that I cannot reach and I ask you to scratch it for me. But, we know that sex is never so simple a matter. The social and psychological significance of things related to sex and sexuality are far more complicated and involved. Our understanding and recognition of sexual desire emerges from the totality of our situation, which is irreducibly communicative. We are aided by understanding sexuality and *erotic perception* in the terms offered by Merleau-Ponty (1962, p. 157): "through one body it aims at another body, and takes place in a world, not in a consciousness." As we begin to develop our descriptions of our lived-experience of sexuality, it is important that we locate ourselves and our sexual experiences within the worlds from which they came to be. It is important that we begin by describing the specific worlds in which we have experienced sexuality and set aside the presumption of what it is, was, or should be.

In the previous chapter, I outlined the three recursive and synergistic steps of semiotic phenomenology. My aim in the present chapter is to provide concrete illustrations of what we actually do in the application of semiotic phenomenology. Because our application of semiotic phenomenology in our communicative sexualities course occurs largely through group work, there is much in the process that is very difficult to fully explicate here. The group work occurs over a sixteen-week period, the last eight of which are often intensive. Group members communicate in person, via asynchronous and synchronous online events, and through the exchange and collective rewriting of the texts produced. My focus here is on how reflection and the cultivation of written texts constitute the application of semiotic phenomenology within the dynamics of the group communication.

SEXUALITIES AS PHENOMENA

What, exactly, is a "phenomenon"? How do we select a "phenomenon" to study? In the colloquial sense, a phenomenon could be anything. We often talk about natural phenomena, like hurricanes or earthquakes. We also commonly use "phenomenon" to describe something like a social fad, something that sweeps over a particular social or cultural group during a particular period of time such that everyone knows about it. For our purposes we will understand a phenomenon as *anything experienced that becomes meaningful.*

Because we are studying phenomena related to sexuality, the phenomenon we select for study must be something experienced that has sexual significance for us. This rather broad designation often provides very little initial guidance for students trying to identify a topic for the research project. But it is important that we don't become too narrow too quickly in our discussion of possible topics. It is important that we begin with a very broad topic that can be recognized as *typical* throughout a cultural or social group, yet specific enough that it can evoke particular moments in time in which this experience and its meaning came into our awareness. Table 7.1 below is a list of possible topics I provide for students).

We must start somewhere, and because we are working phenomenologically, the attention must focus on human experience and the meaningfulness of that experience. In order to decide on your general topic, you should listen to each other talk about your interests and experiences. Try to make

Table 7.1. List of Possible Topics Related to Sexuality

Possible Topics for Research on Sexuality	
Experience of sexual desire	Experience of sexual regret
Experience of sexual vulnerability	Experience of sexual fulfillment
Experience of sexual uncertainty	Experience of sexual power
Experience of having sexual power or wanting power over another	Experience of being wanted by the other more than wanting the other or the reverse
Experience of having sexual desire that is at odds with social expectations	Experience of being or wanting to be sexually overpowered
Experience of questioning one's sexual desire	Experience of sexual difference
Experience of saying "no" or not being able to say "no" to sexual activity	Experience of not being "seen," or of being "misunderstood" in a sexual context
Experience of "masculine" sexuality	Experience of being sexually "objectified"
Experience of "feminine" sexuality	Experience of having a diseased sexual body

connections between and among yourselves, share your ideas, and identify something that seems to interest all of you.

Selecting a phenomenon must involve a process of intuitive guessing. Because we are working in groups, the experiences of each of the group members will be central to discovering the phenomenon to study. You must listen carefully to each other and seek to discover experiences that are common, or that intersect, or in some way have a likeness or alliance with each other. Selecting a phenomenon must involve a process of direction by discovery. Working with partners or in groups is often helpful because it gives the opportunity for us to listen to ourselves and others. In this listening, we can discover aspects of our experience that we were not aware of previously. The phenomenon you will come to study must *emerge*. Once you have a general idea of the phenomenon you want to study, you must remain *oriented toward* it without closing out the possibility of it changing. In fact, if the phenomenon you initially chose to study does not change over the course of your study, then your study will have in some sense failed to locate experience as a process. As you describe your experiences and listen to each other, you must be able to suspend your initial perception and understanding so that you can come to see the differences that emerge among all of you. You must draw a fine balance between being open to all the manifestations of the experience and being overly focused and closing off your access to those manifestations. Conducting phenomenological interviews is the major practice through which we will work. The duel challenge of being open, yet focused, will present itself strongly in the interviewing process.

Once you have a general idea of your topic, then you need to begin to explore it as a phenomenon. You should do this within your group by discussing *what it is* that comes to mind for each of you when you think about your selected topic. It is common to actually change or modify your original topic after you begin researching it. Your discussion will inevitably focus you more strongly on the phenomenon you are considering.

Understanding the Essence of Sexualities as Phenomena

Phenomenological research is concerned with the meaningfulness of lived-experience, that is, its typicality. It studies the "phenomena" of experience and attempts to discover the "structural invariants" or "essential structures" that make particular experiences possible. As a "logic of phenomena," the research is concerned with the "universal" aspects of experience (experience types) as they are manifested in the particular experience of a particular person (experiences tones). People are unique and therefore have many idiosyncrasies or peculiarities (tonality). Phenomenologically, it is important to differentiate between those idiosyncrasies and aspects of experience that are essential to a given phenomenon as it is typical within a specific cultural time and place (i.e., a typification). The effort to explicate the "essential structures" of a phenomenon is very different from "essential-izing" the phenomenon that we study. It is very important that we remember that the study of lived-experience, and our effort to understand what could be universal about that lived-experience, is to identify "structural invariants" that make it possible for the phenomenon to appear as it did. To identify these "structural invariants" is not to offer a definition upon which we claim the existence of some immutable truth. Rather, it is to identify the conditions of possibility through which the experience of a particular phenomenon became real as a *typification* of a *typology* (Lanigan, 1992, p. 216).

Every human being is born into culture at a specific historical moment and in a specific location. As a result, we inherit specific facts of language, social institutions (social structure), history, and practices (ways of doing as prescribed by our culture). As we exist within the specifics of this situation, we have experiences. These experiences are social and lived-through, hence become the preferences we embody as members of our culture. That is to say that even our most private experience is enabled by the fact that we exist within the specifics of our situation. The combination of culture and experience is what gives us our ever-evolving and dynamic sense of *self* as a person and the world as we live in it—we develop a certain body (both the actual physical body and our body-image—i.e., our feeling about our body), with certain habits, preferences, and a certain style, none of which can be reduced either to the norms of culture or the idiosyncrasies of experience. All of these relationships are dynamic, interdependent, and mutually reconstructive aspects of these relationships.

There are many advantages to taking a phenomenological approach to the teaching and researching that define communicative sexualities. First and foremost, a phenomenological approach commits us to an examination of the lived-world in which we all come to experience what we experience. As such, a phenomenological approach requires a disciplined, direct, and honest examination of the facts of our experience as they are experienced without the heavy hand of our taken-for-granted presumptions about the nature of reality dominating our seeing, feeling, and thinking. In living through our everyday worlds as human beings, our seeing and thinking is ordinary, normal, and familiar. I don't have to think twice when I feel pleasure in noticing the attractiveness of another person's body, or when I am repulsed by a vulgar comment made toward me. I am simply living my life, going about my everyday affairs and noticing my responses to various things I encounter. This is what phenomenologists call the "natural attitude"—our ordinary attitude toward the world which is my conscious experience. Yet, as human beings we exist within a complex of cultural, social, personal, and biological forces that are far more present and involved than our ordinary seeing and thinking ever takes account of. Why I find this particular body attractive, or am repulsed by that particular comment, is not just a consequence of some idiosyncrasy of my own self, but is, rather, strongly related to the social and cultural worlds in which I was reared and live, my histories within those worlds. What becomes present to us in our conscious awareness is always only a small part of the totality of the reality in which we live and come to experience.

CULTIVATING RESEARCH CAPTA
AND DISCOVERING PHENOMENA

Semiotic phenomenology, like all research practice, is conducted in situ. The scientist is a person who, however technologically aided, must decide what is relevant, must interpret results, and must assign significance. The primary tools of the semiotic phenomenologist are speech and language, consciousness and experience. Audio-video recordings of behavior, transcriptions of speech, and written texts produced through interviews and reflection on all these capta provide the semiotic phenomenologist with important resources for examining the phenomenon in question. It is important that we recognize the differences in the capacities of speech as spoken and heard, language as written and read, and gesture as expressed and perceived. All of these modalities of communication are crucial: each provides a reflective, reflexive, and reversible context for the other. The application of semiotic phenomenology in my communicative sexualities course focuses on the dynamic process between that which is spoken and heard, that which is written and read, and that which is perceived and expressed—the very juncture of self and other.

The primary tool we use in our semiotic phenomenological research is the phenomenological interview. We will listen to each other talk about our sexual experience with a particular focus on the immediate and concrete circumstances through which the experience came to have the meaning it did for us. We will examine the process of topical protocol interviewing and its function within the three major methodological steps of semiotic phenomenology. It is important to remember that as we go through this process we are inevitably stepping into a process of meaning construction that is already at work. There is no "pristine" state of experience that stands as the object of our recollections and speech. Our effort is to be faithful to experience as we experienced it, but the path to faithfulness is in its creation.

Once each group of students has selected a topic for study, the students conduct one-on-one phenomenological interviews with each other about the phenomenon they have selected. On the basis of these interviews, the interviewer then produces a phenomenological description (or narrative) of the experience in which the phenomenon is thought to exist. In addition to conducting these interviews, each student must write his own description (or narrative) of his experience—the same one he talked about when he was interviewed. As a result, we end up with two descriptions of each student's experience—the one he wrote (a Self perspective), and the one produced by his interviewer (an Other perspective). The results of this exercise are virtually always the same—the narrative text produced by the interviewer is better, clearer, and more focused on the immediate and concrete experience than the one the student produced for himself.

As we examine the difference between the two descriptions, we discover the many subtle and not so subtle ways in which we are invested in a particular "reading," or "rationale," of our own experience. In comparing these two versions of our own experience, we see how our writing about our experience privileges a particular investment or orientation toward that experience that clearly shades the description itself (i.e., an unintended "idealization"). We are able to recognize this because we see the ways in which the language used in the interviewer's description, provides in fact, a better, more direct, and accurate account (i.e., an intended "realization) of our own experience. In completing this exercise, we have begun to break through what we presume is the transparency of our own speech and language, and we have experienced a successful invocation of the phenomenological epochē (bracketing). As a result of reading my interviewer's description, I can now see how my own descriptions are constrained with my own interpretive priorities. Because I now see this constraint, I can bracket it and look again at my experience and the phenomenon I think is located within it.

This initial exercise is very important because it is natural to presume that we are able to describe our experience in a way that is completely accurate and transparent to our own understanding. It is inevitable, however, that as we begin a process of engaging sustained variations and reflections related to our *experience*, we come to discover much that eluded or remained hidden to us in our original rendition. As the group itself engages this process through a series of sustained variations and reflections related to the *phenomena*, we begin to discover a much larger and more detailed account of the phenomenon itself and our experience of it. Through this process, the group modifies and adjusts its understanding of what it is studying, transforming it into a more precise and nuanced phenomenon.

Some of the most common topics initially selected by students over the many years I have taught communicative sexualities include the experience of losing one's virginity, the experience of sexual regret, and the experience of sexual desire. As these topics evolve during the research process, the topic of "sexual desire," for example, can turn into "sexual desire and initiation," or "sexual desire outside of a relationship," or "fulfillment of sexual desire." All of the topics undergo significant change over the course of the research project as the students recognize the complex sets of convergences and divergences among their varied experiences. Although some of the originally selected topics are better suited to phenomenological analysis than others, it is most important at the beginning stages of the research that students identify specific experiences that fit generally under the topic the group has chosen. If they cannot find a topic that allows each of them to focus fully on the lived-reality of their experience, then no matter how "good" the topic, the research will never succeed.

Consider the following example. During the initial discussion of possible topics, one student group was having difficulty finding something on which they could all agree. I joined their discussion and began asking questions that helped them "flesh out" more of the details of their own experiences related to the topics they were considering. It is often the case that when we first compare two different experiences, they appear so different that we cannot imagine any possible connection. One person in the group had suggested studying "the experience of a sexual threesome." This topic was problematical for the group because everyone presumed that a "threesome" involves three people (bodies) engaged in sexual activity together. Not everyone in this group had this particular experience. But as they talked about it more and suspended the presupposition that a "threesome" must involve three bodies, they began to see a phenomenon of "third person present."

What began as an initial rejection of the topic now evolved into something with which the members of the group felt much more connected from within their own experience. One group member described the experience of having sex with a new partner shortly after ending a previous relationship wherein both partners retained some affection for each other. The person from their previous relationship remained a very strong presence in the actual immediacy of the new sexual encounter. The new sexual partner was literally experienced side by side with the affection and memory of the previous partner, and the relative satisfaction of the new sexual encounter was experienced only in direct comparison to the previous partner. Another student experienced a similar situation, but because the relationship had ended badly, a lot of anger remained and greatly affected the new sexual experience itself. We came to discover that the anger was so strong that the desire to find sexual satisfaction in the new encounter was literally driven by a feeling of "showing" the previous partner just how much he or she was "over" the previous relationship.

The group also discovered that a "threesome" can emerge when one is having sex with one person but imagines or wishes that a different person were present, and for this person the experience itself was filtered through the back-and-forth of what was actually present and what was imagined. In one variation of this experience, a feeling of guilt for wanting and imagining the person other than the one present intervened in the body's presence with its sexual energy. The person who felt this guilt had been criticized for having any sexual attention directed toward or inspired by anything outside of the primary relationship. The guilt and self-censoring that resulted greatly diminished the degree of immersion and presence in the sexual activity itself. On those occasions when the guilt could be set aside, however, the imagined partner heightened the immediate sexual immersion because the wanting of the person not present cultivated strong sexual energies.

Even in the case of the three bodies engaging in sexual activity, the descriptions of experience revealed that the "third person"—the one who came into the dyad at the request of one member of the dyad—was very much a "third person" who was variously integrated into the sexual practices familiar to the other two persons. Of course, that "integration" was anything but clear or straightforward, especially if the desire to experience the threesome resulted from one person in the dyad persuading the other to go along. In the case of one student, who was in a heterosexual relationship where her male partner persuaded her to bring another female into the sexual relationship, the struggle was in seeing her boyfriend having intercourse with this new woman. Although she had "mentally prepared" herself for seeing this, and imagined finding it a bit of a turn-on, the actual feeling of being "left out" while the other two were having intercourse was difficult for her to deal with. In a different case, the threesome was initiated by the female of the heterosexual couple who had found herself attracted to another woman. The male partner of this couple did not need much persuading to agree to this liaison, but the interest of the female partner tended more toward a female-female dyad experience than a threesome experience. The implications for the primary dyad relationship were thusly affected.

Each of these cases of "third person present" has significant differences, yet it was possible to locate a phenomenon of *competing awareness* wherein their usual attention to themselves and their sexual partner is at odds with this new (or old) sexual partner and the self it allows to emerge. The resulting uncertainty emerges because the "third person present" allows for a literal switch between the two possible "others" through which the "self" is experienced. With each switch in attention the consequence for seeing and experiencing the self changes, and very different experience emerges than could in a purely dyadic encounter. The group found a phenomenon of "third person present" that emerged in such a way that they could constitute it as the topic of their research. It is in this way that we recognize the coherence of a phenomenon that is not unique or located solely within the psychological disposition of a single person, but rather is shared by cultural groups in which the sexual dyad constitutes the normative condition. Whether the "third person present" was an actual physical body or an imagined presence, the phenomena showed a high degree of coherence. The "essential structure" of the "third person present" phenomenon entailed an "interruption" or "competition" in the self-other dyad in which varying adjustments in the perception of the other and expressions of the self became new objects of awareness and required an explicit rethinking of the primary dyadic relationship.

This brief illustration summarizes in large part the recursive and synergistic nature of semiotic phenomenology as a research methodology which produces *description* as a research outcome.

EXPLICATING MEANING

When we seek to discover what it is that made it possible to have had the experience that we did, we mean this quite literally—not in the sense that, well, I had to have the car, and I had to be able to get off work, so we had to be able to coordinate our schedules. No, those kinds of details help provide a context for experience, but they do not make our experiencing possible. In order to discover what made it possible for us to have had the experience that we did, we must look at the very sign-system and processes through which we *ascribe significance and create meaning* within the experiencing itself. What, exactly, does this mean? Consider the following examples.

A common topic for students to consider when they begin looking at their experience of sexuality is the "experience of losing one's virginity." When students begin to reflect on this experience it usually entails some description of their experience of the actual act itself, as in these examples:

- "I didn't know if I was doing it right."
- "I kept expecting it to hurt, but it didn't."
- "I just wanted to get it done and get out of there."
- "I kept thinking about how I was going to be able to tell my friends that I finally did it."
- "I had planned it all to be very romantic, but it was really just awkward."

Each of these statements reveal something about the sign-systems through which these particular students made sense of a particular sexual encounter. Regardless of the particulars of each experience, we can see how the statements themselves reveal various elements of significance that were necessary for the experience to have been described in this way. To say "I didn't know if I was doing it right" could only be articulated as an experience if one had a sense that it could be done "wrong." Not everyone who engages in sexual activity for the first time feels strongly enough about doing it "right" or "wrong" so that this becomes a major feature of the actual experience itself.

The statement "I kept expecting it to hurt, but it didn't" seems obviously gendered female and reflects our cultural knowledge that for a woman to be penetrated for the first time is to be physically violated in having her hymen pierced. Yet, we know that not all women experience pain during their first intercourse. Moreover, people experience their bodies differently, especially when it comes to pain. Male students in my classes have also described experiencing pain that seems to be associated with the awkwardness of their first intercourse. Finally, there is a fine line between the pain/pleasure threshold, and as the intensity of any physical activity increases we often become less sensitive to pain and sometimes even inspired or motivated by it in a way that makes it pleasurable.

Consider now the next two statements: "I wanted to just get it done and get out of there" and "I kept thinking about how I was going to be able to tell my friends that I finally did it." Each of these statements reveals a strong concern with matters less connected to the fact of the body's experience than the previous ones. For the students who made these statements, their expectations about having "done it" governed much of what they experience during the immediacy of their experience of losing their virginity. Wanting to just "get it done" could apply to many things in life, and across the board this statement signifies an urgency to complete the act and move on to other things. The fact that these words apply to one's experience of losing one's virginity points to priorities other than physical pleasure.

The next statement, "I kept thinking about how I was going to be able to tell my friends that I finally did it," seems to make what could be implicit in the previous statement explicit. The idea that one wants to get it done and get out of there seems to be part of the same signifying system that includes "to be able to tell my friends that I finally did it." After all, we are not talking about using a toilet and running out to the car so one can continue a road trip. To have experienced losing one's virginity as described in these two statements reflects strongly the importance of the status "not a virgin" within one's social group. Both statements seems to reveal that the particulars of the situation, including the other person, the physical feelings, or notions of having "become a man" or "become a woman" by losing one's virginity, all lack significance compared to the mere fact of having completed the act.

The final statement, "I had planned it all to be very romantic, but it was really just awkward," is a good example of how strongly our ideals can come to define the very reality we come to experience. Perhaps it is true that all first experiences of sexuality with another person are "awkward" just by comparison to subsequent experiences. We wouldn't necessarily have described our first experience as "awkward" except for having subsequent experiences that allow us to see the "awkwardness" of the first. If, on the other hand, we hold clear and strong sets of expectations associated with a blissful ease of "true love" and "romance," "awkwardness" becomes easily experienced. Whenever I see student descriptions that are filled with abstract idealization about love and romance, I know that the student has yet to look directly at the immediacy of his or her experience.

That is not to say that I think the student is insincere or lying, but that even in a context where we accept that "true love" and "romance" defined much of the experience, the actual experiencing involves much more than that. It is most certainly the case that even if my greatest aspirations for human connection were realized, there was much more going on than a simple fulfillment of what I expected. What were the surprises? What did each person learn about the other? What had to be overcome to reach that feeling of intimate human connection? Whatever one's experience was that led to describing it as an expression of "true love" has many particulars to it. A scenario that leaves me feeling as though I have had the ultimate possible experience of human connection and love is unlikely to work the same for any other person. If we fail to examine those differences and allow ourselves to remain taken within the comfort and security of our ideals, then we will never be able to reflect on the concrete and immediate terms and conditions that have made our experiencing possible.

CONCLUSION

My effort in this chapter has been to illustrate key aspects of semiotic phenomenology as applied. The examples in this chapter have been taken directly from work done by students in my Communicative Sexualities class. It is important to understand the nature of phenomena as they are studied phenomenologically, and the essential link between the researchers and the phenomenon as it emerges in the application of semiotic phenomenology. The invocation of the epochē, the cultivation of capta, and the explication of meaning must be engaged in the practice of the research itself. It is impossible to fully anticipate the results of this practice, yet these results can never be separated from the particular people doing the research. The only way we can assess the adequacy and accuracy of the results of this research application is through a return to the person wherein a new examination of the phenomenon has been made possible. What at first seemed relatively straightforward and obvious is revealed to be complexly intertwined with the specifics of time, place, and culture as they are at work within the conscious experience of the researchers themselves. As these complexities are revealed, we recognize cultural typifications as they are present across what we might have thought of as disparate experiences, and thus also travel the large distances present in our experiencing that we otherwise would never have seen.

FOR FURTHER READING

Jacqueline M. Martinez, *Phenomenology of Chicana Experience and Identity: Communication and Transformation in Praxis* (Lanham, Md.: Rowman & Littlefield, 2000).

Jacqueline M. Martinez, "Weight Room Semiotics: Female Bodies Enacting Masculine Codes," *The American Journal of Semiotics*, vol. 17, no. 4 (Winter 2001): 147–73.

William R. McKenna, "Epochē and Reduction," in *Encyclopedia of Phenomenology*, ed. Lester Embree et al. (Dordrecht: Kluwer Academic Publishers, 1997), 177–80.

8

Cultural Ethics and Personal Obligations

To focus on the direct and specific experiences of sexuality in the lives of twenty to thirty people who will be working together in the same classroom over the course of a sixteen-week semester requires a great deal of maturity and self-confidence among all those involved. It also requires a great deal of pedagogical precision by any person attempting to teach such a class. Any person leading students through the emphatically personal and intimate terrain of this kind of course must be accountable to 1) their own abilities and limitations with regard to their own personal history of sexual experience, 2) their awareness of social and cultural preferences or biases that are inevitably present in themselves and their students, and 3) their ability to create a fundamentally safe, open, positive, and affirming environment in which everyone in the classroom can come to work successfully together in genuinely human ways. Over the past several years of teaching this course, I have been especially concerned with the responsibilities that come with teaching a course that aims for students to be direct and explicit about their immediate and lived-experiences of sexuality.

Throughout this work I have emphasized the many challenges involved in suspending our presuppositions, especially as they function at the cultural level of communication. It can be very difficult—perhaps never really fully possible—to accurately assess the difference between a more successful and less successful suspension of any specific presupposition. My emphasis on the philosophical orientation of communicology and its methodological practice of semiotic phenomenology provides a robust and demanding process through which we can be more confident in our assertions about successful suspension of presuppositions. Even still, it has been my experience that it is sometimes the case that the most theoretically oriented students are less capable of successfully applying semiotic phenomenology precisely because they tend to be so focused on the intellectual effort. In other words, the effort to "master" the theory can sometimes allow one to avoid looking directly at the fact of her or his experience. This tendency also appears with students who are most comfortable being in complete control of their own written language. Sometimes these students tend toward a more poetic extreme where their investment in the elegance of their language limits their ability to examine their experience in new ways. Other times these students tend toward an analytic precision where their investment in accuracy in their language and expression creates a distance between them and their experience that also limits their ability to see in new ways.

The best way to counter these tendencies to control our expressions and thus limit our access to the immediacy of experience is through a process of listening to others as they describe their own experiences as they are both similar to and different from one's own. This is the process of imaginative variation, and our capacity to listen to each other in ways that allow us to see what was there in the immediacy of our experience, yet beyond our ability to articulate, is the most important moment in the application of semiotic phenomenology in the study of our lived-experience of sexuality.

Nothing happens in a classroom except through the influence of the teacher. The only way for teachers to cultivate the kind of engagement that can lead to a genuine discovery of the fact of our lived-experience of sexuality is to model that very kind of engagement. Thus, the teacher's ability to hear, describe, and offer variations upon what the students say in the classroom and bring in their written work is the most important factor in one's capacity to lead students through the process of researching lived-experience of sexuality. The teacher's personal experience of sexuality, and her or his life history contextualizing this experience, are inevitably at work in how this process unfolds in the classroom. This fact offers both the most severe limitation and most important means through which a teacher conducts the kind of class I have been detailing throughout this work. Communicology requires that we take the presence of the human being as essential and irreducible in the emergence of lived-experience. Teachers cannot delude themselves into thinking that they can separate themselves from their own biases and prejudices. Rather, the teacher must be the leader in illustrating how one takes account of those very biases and prejudices in ways that further the process of discovery. Both an advanced theoretical understanding and a rigorously applied research process are required in order to cultivate this capacity for hearing and seeing beyond what one is initially capable of. My effort has been to illustrate how the application of semiotic phenomenology cultivates this capacity.

The reader will have noticed that I have focused this work on U.S. American culture. I have emphasized how the particular tendency within U.S. American culture to revere individuality and assert autonomy in relation to other people and the circumstances in which one lives limits our ability to study those very interconnections that make our own sense of individuality and autonomy possible. This point is especially important in the transition from adolescence to adulthood, particularly because this is the time when young people are expected to develop a heightened sense of their sexual selves. There is no doubt that the influence of peers, and the unspoken yet powerfully present expectations of family, community, and culture, come strongly to bear at this time in life. To be under the heavy influence of a social world, yet to deny the existence of that influence, reduces one's ability to ascertain exactly what and how one experiences oneself in conjunction with those influences. Whatever the cultural context in which a class such as Communicative Sexualities is taught, the teacher must have already traversed the vast cultural terrain across which students have traveled and will come to travel. This does not make the teacher "expert," or somehow omniscient regarding students' experience. Rather, it allows the teacher to demonstrate how the connections between history, time, and context that are at work in the emergence of experience, and as we examine the fact of our lived-experience. I have also found it to be true that the greater my capacity to bring these connections to light, the more I learn about these connections as they are at work in U.S. American culture. There is no book or account of culture that better reveals its content and presence than the particular and dynamic communication that occurs when we collectively struggle to hear and understand ourselves and others. Communicology, and its methodology of semiotic phenomenology, provide the logic and practice through which this can be achieved in a rigorous, systematic, and scientific way.

The kind of awareness and knowledge required to create a fundamentally safe, open, positive, and affirming pedagogical environment is not a matter of having reached a certain "end point" in self-awareness or knowledge. Rather, it is a matter of mature, honest, and open engagement with the realities of who one is and how one lives—that is, with who and what we bring, exactly and precisely, into that classroom each and every time we step into it. It is a rather tall order, especially considering that for most college teachers it is our specific field of expertise that defines our presence in the classroom and provides a consistent, firm, and reliable base upon which we can return again and again in our relatedness to the work we are asking the students to perform in the class.

Teaching Communicative Sexualities is different from this normative situation of college teaching in that the specific subject matter of the class—the fact and reality of sexual experiences of those of us in the class that will come to be studied—is not set in its specifics a priori. What is set a priori, and thus provides a consistent, firm, safe, and reliable base which guides the work we asking the students to perform, is a commitment to the theoretical and methodological priorities of communicology and semiotic phenomenology. We must not be satisfied with our taken-for-granted presumptions about what sexuality is or should be. We must, in every case, be committed to an open and thoroughgoing search for the complexities of our thinking and feeling as they are related to the immediacy of our lived-experiences of sexuality.

It is impossible to provide a list of specifics about how the kind of commitment I am advocating becomes manifest in the immediacy of the classroom experience. The study of communicology and application of semiotic phenomenology aid significantly in this effort. In the end, however, it is the teacher and students—the real-life embodied persons—as present and mutually engaged in the immediacy of communication within the class that determine the quality of the class thus conducted. I have tried, throughout this work, to provide examples that illustrate the unfolding of this commitment within classroom communication. Even the best theory and most detailed practice can be corrupted in its application. Communication, like sexuality, has a dual potential of becoming an experience that is edifying and enriching, or alienating and dismissive.

AMBIGUITY, CONTINGENCY, AND SPEECH-SPEAKING

This dynamic of teaching and learning that supports a deeply human process of examining the fact of our lived-experience of sexuality requires ambiguity and contingency. To reject ambiguity or contingency is to necessarily presume that one knows what is present in advance of experience and communication. None of us can say what exactly will make the difference between a fundamentally safe, open, positive, and affirming classroom and one that is not. Over the past several years of teaching Communicative Sexualities, I have recognized some commonalities across classes that seem to cultivate a fundamental sense of maturity and respect. But, no matter how real these commonalities, I am also always surprised because something new and different occurs in every class. I find that I must be very attuned to the specific students of each class and their expressions as they emerge in the immediacy of our communication.

To achieve the kind of engagement I am calling for here means that we move beyond the sedimented routines of the normative ways we talk about sex—that is, we must move beyond what Merleau-Ponty refers to as "speech-spoken" (Merlau-Ponty, 1962/1945, p. 178). We must be able and willing to hear ourselves speak, to hear our own voice in others, and hear their voice in ours. This means that we must cultivate the capacity to attend to the body and the body's experience. Speaking and listening must be understood far beyond the notion of content. We must come to engage speech (speaking) as gesture and embodiment. Our bodies carry knowledge.

Our bodies are not "imprinted" in any static sense—even in the case of trauma, where the experience of the "present" collapses and the body's memory of a past traumatic experience becomes devastatingly present, that past that becomes present is linked in some way or another to a trigger or some sequence of events in the original present. Our bodies are bearers of the factual realities of our lives, the cumulative factual realities of our lives. These factual realities become varyingly present within specific contexts and experiences of communication. Far above and separate from whatever conscious stories we might tell about our life histories, our bodies have their own particular recollections that can never align fully with our conscious thought. As we cultivate a relationship with our bodies that engenders a sensitivity to gesture, we begin to open the potential for self-knowledge that can make a tremendous difference in our personal and collective lives. This kind of sensitivity can become freeing in the sense that we become more rooted, grounded, and connected to the reality of our experiencing. We are less led astray by the many external, often illusory, and superficially gratifying norms and practices of our contemporary mass society.

I think it is accurate to say that in our contemporary mass society we are immersed within messages that portray beauty and sexual desirability in very narrow and consistent terms. I am not going to make an explicit critique about this standard of beauty and sexual desirability, but I think it is important to point out that the more we embrace the narrow and static terms of beauty and sexual desirability as presented in mass media, the more limited we are in discovering beauty and sexual desirability in the many complex and dynamic expressions we encounter in ourselves and others. The pursuit of beauty or love as a human being is complex and requires a complex pursuit. Merely owning an object, occupying an object, or acquiring all of superficial accoutrements to meet that ideal or portray that ideal is insufficient to reach the level of human achievement.

CULTURAL ETHICS AND PERSONAL OBLIGATIONS BEYOND THE CLASSROOM

We are all very aware that attitudes about sexuality vary widely within our current social and cultural environment. Issues related to sexuality are at the root of many of our most polarizing and decisive political battles. Gay marriage, birth control and reproductive rights, stem cell research, the "don't ask, don't tell" policy of the United States military, sex education in public schools, and the like are in many cases litmus tests for political contests ranging from Supreme Court nominees and presidential elections, all the way down to local school boards. The much publicized sexual oppression exacted by the Taliban against women provided a strong public relations point through which the United States sought justification for military intervention in sovereign countries. Issues related to social "safety nets," like welfare and food stamps, are often criticized on the false presumption that people (almost always portrayed and assumed to be black) on welfare and/or who receive food stamps are happy to live sexually promiscuous lives which allows them to bear more children and live off of taxpayers' money.

At the same time, fertility-enhancing technologies have made the production of quadruplets and so on almost common. This birthing of "multiples" is often celebrated in news accounts that feature the "courage" and "faith" that these families (almost always white and middle to upper middle class) have in facing these multiple births and call for public support and donations to aid these families. We are entertained by *Jon and Kate plus Eight*, and thereby tacitly support the making of a family life into a public carnival that keeps the roof over their head and food in the pantry. The exploitation of children by their parents' deliberate choice to display them through public spectacle now appears to many as a legitimate option for generating family income.

The exponential growth in our use of technology, especially among younger generations, makes it possible for sexual displays on mass scales. With a simple cell phone girls can visually record various kinds of flirtations that run the entire gamut from mere suggestion, to displays of nudity, to full-on exposure of sexual acts. Within a matter of seconds, they can make that recording available to millions of Internet users. For many, this is considered "just fun." But it seems clear that many of the girls and young women who come to make these recordings do so because of the social context of drunkenness and their own vulnerabilities to the suggestiveness of peers. It seems clear that many of them often come later to regret it deeply. There is often a fine line between a healthy assertion of one's own sexual presence and a self-exploitation of one's sexuality for the titillations or financial benefits of oneself and others.

The work I have pursued here aims to make it clear that these "fine" (and sometimes not so "fine") lines between a healthy assertion of one's sexuality and self and other exploitive assertions of sexuality mark some very complex points of convergence and divergence among cultural, social, historical, and personal forces, interests, and awarenesses. Given the complex and dynamic nature of these convergences and divergences, it is simply not possible to effectively regulate and thereby cultivate sexual standards or values by public decree. No written law or policy can ever instantiate the values that motivate its construction by mere fact of its creation. No punishment thus legitimated via that law or policy can reach into the immediacy of lived-experience and alter the sense-making and active negotiation of social and cultural pressures each of us undertakes in the course of our everyday lives. We cannot, in other words, invoke an ethic that can stand its charge in light of these complex points of convergence and divergence unless we begin with the fact and circumstance of embodied human experience.

Yet, I do not believe that we can or should abandon the effort to establish common notions of what constitutes "good" and "bad" sex, or "good" and "bad" laws or policies related to sexuality and sexual practices, or even just "good" or "bad" ideas about sexuality. Our obligations to those generations that have preceded us and those that will follow us is too great to succumb to a nihilistic attitude. Sexual and interpersonal violence within intimate relationships sustains cycles of violence within families and across generations. As a society we live in the midst of many such families, and, in some cases, even such communities. Sexuality alone is not the only factor at work here, and cultivating healthy sexual relationships and healthy intimacy within families that can extend to the level of community is affected also by economic conditions, educational opportunities, and other tangible resources that are and are not available to families and communities. Sexuality may be just one factor among many, but make no mistake about it, it is a very, very important factor.

It is difficult to know exactly what can make the difference in turning human communities that perpetuate cycles of relational and sexual violence into human communities that have the capacity to sustain the recognition and acknowledgment of human life through all of the contingencies and ambiguities that confront us endlessly as we move through the moments of our personal and collective lives. I do think, however, that when we come to understand what happens on an interpersonal level when a person is able to undertake the radical change required to extricate oneself from a violent relationship, we can discover qualities of communication as it engenders a self-understanding that can also help alleviate tendencies toward violence at the group and cultural levels of communication.

Adults who come to have humanly enriching long-term relationships know that this achievement involves many sequences of ups and downs, of better and worse times, of sometimes more and sometimes less successful intimacy. The discovery of life-affirming sexual practices is rarely simple, obvious, or easily sustained amidst the complexities of interpersonal, familial, and community relationships. Sometimes what begin as profoundly life-affirming sexual practices paradoxically become non-life affirming. The ambiguities and contingencies of communication and relationship development, coupled with our culture's narrow and static representations of sexuality, make any such straightforward achievement of life-affirming sexual practice that is sustainable over the course of a lifetime difficult to achieve. The ideals of love, beauty, and sexual appeal as cultivated in mass media rarely communicate the reality of struggle and achievement that goes hand in hand with the pursuit of any ideal, personal, social, or cultural.

Throughout this work I have emphasized my fundamental belief that sex is inherently good, and that when human beings seek fulfillment of sexual desire within human relationships, that in and of itself entails the possibility of the highest achievements of human intimacy, mutual respect, and acknowledgment. When sex becomes exploitive or humanly degrading is not because sexual desire itself exists as a fact of being human. Rather, it is because we have failed to cultivate a strong enough sense of human intimacy and connection across all aspects of personal, interpersonal, social, and cultural life. We cannot change the terms and conditions of our interrelations with other human beings absent a willingness to examine the reality of our experience *prior to* the instantiation of any rules or laws. I may live much of my adult life in an abusive or unhealthy relationship and do it "for the benefit of the kids." Yet, the fact that I do this means that my children are exposed to the habits and dispositions perpetuated with the abusive or unhealthy relationship that they see in their parents every day. Children learn what they live far more than what they are told, and so it is with human communities. Ideals and possibilities do not always match up.

I am not saying one's decision to stay in a married relationship for the sake of one's children is necessarily the wrong or a bad choice, or that I somehow know what it would take to make the totality of a social situation equate to the greatest degree of health and well-being of all those within it. My point is, rather, that this kind of rationale, wherein our attention evades examination of the immediate and concrete circumstances in which we come to both experience and meaning, encourages us to think that how we *actually live* in relationships—how we embody the concrete interactions of our daily lives—can be kept or stopped from influencing or affecting the lives of those with whom we are interconnected. It cannot.

This ability to gain greater access to actually live within the concreted and embodied interactions of our daily lives is what I think should be an essential part of any kind of "sex education." A commitment to a careful examination of the human presence that is immediately entailed in any and every moment of human experience should be an important part of all education. As a culture we do not cultivate the kinds of awarenesses that are required for us to be able to take seriously and examine directly our human presence in the immediacy of our human lives. Moreover, we live with educational institutions that place a very high premium on an objectified knowledge that is "objective" precisely because it succeeds at removing or neutralizing the fact of our human presence. Objectivity is not a goal to be diminished or discarded. At the same time, however, we must recognize the severity of the challenges entailed in ascertaining what human objectivity is with regard to what is lived and embodied in the sexuality of our human existence. We must set ourselves toward reaching that conscious understanding in the process of communicating within ourselves and to others.

FOR FURTHER READING

Lewis Gordon, *Disciplinary Decadence: Living Thought in Trying Times* (Boulder, Colo.: Paradigm Publishers, 2006).

Richard Lanigan, "Urban Crisis: The Phenomenology of Social Polarization and Communication," in *Phenomenology of Communication: Merleau-Ponty's Thematics in Communicology and Semiology* (Pittsburgh, Pa.: Duquesne University Press, 1988), 134–43.

Elizabeth Ströker, "Evidence," in *Encyclopedia of Phenomenology*, ed. Lester Embree et al. (Boston: Kluwer Academic Publishers, 1997), 202–4.

Works Cited

Beauvoir, Simone de. *The Second Sex*. New York: Vintage Books, 1989/1952.

Fausto-Sterling, Ann. *Sexing the Body: Gender Politics and the Construction of Sexuality*. New York: Basic Books, 2000.

Holenstein, Elmar. *Roman Jakobson's Approach to Language: Phenomenological Structuralism*. Bloomington, Ind.: Indiana University Press, 1974.

Ihde, D. *Experimental Phenomenology: An Introduction*. Albany, N.Y.: State University of New York Press, 1997.

Jakobson, R. *On Language*, ed. L. R. Waugh & M. Monville-Burston. Cambridge, Mass.: Harvard University Press, 1990.

Kaplan, A. *The Conduct of Inquiry: Methodology for Behavioral Science*. New Brunswick: Transaction Publishers, 1998/1964.

Kristeva, Julia. *Revolution in Poetic Language*. New York: Columbia University Press, 1984.

———. "The System and the Speaking Subject," in *The Kristeva Reader*, ed. Toril Moi. New York: Columbia University Press, 1986.

Lanigan, Richard L. *Speaking and Semiology: Maurice Merleau-Ponty's Phenomenological Theory of Existential Communication*, 2nd ed. New York: Mouton de Gruyter, 1991/1972.

———. *Speech Act Phenomenology*. The Hague: Martinus Nijhoff, 1977.

———. *Semiotic Phenomenology of Rhetoric: Eidetic Practice in Henry Grattan's Discourse on Tolerance*. Washington, D.C.: The Center for Advanced Research in Phenomenology and University Press of America, 1984.

———. *Phenomenology of Communication: Merleau-Ponty's Thematics in Communicology and Semiology*. Pittsburgh, Pa.: Duquesne University Press, 1988.

———. *The Human Science of Communicology: A Phenomenology of Discourse in Foucault and Merleau-Ponty*. Pittsburgh, Pa.: Duquesne University Press, 1992.

————. "Communicology," in International Encyclopedia of Communication (12 vols), ed. Wolfgang Donsbach. Oxford, UK, and Malden, Mass.: Wiley-Blackwell Publishing Co.,: International Communication Association, vol. 3, 2008.

Leeds-Hurwitz, W. *Semiotics and Communication: Signs, Codes, Cultures*. Hillsdale, N.J.: Lawrence Erlbaum Associates, Publishers, 1993.

Lévi-Strauss, C. *The Elementary Structures of Kinship*, trans. J. H. Bell and J. von Strumer. Boston: Beacon Press, 1969/1949.

Martinez, Jacqueline M. *Phenomenology of Chicana Experience and Identity: Communication and Transformation in Praxis*. Lanham, Md.: Rowman & Littlefield, 2000.

————. "Racisms, Heterosexisms, Identities: A Semiotic Phenomenology of Self Understanding." *Journal of Homosexuality*, 45(2/3) (2003): 109–27.

————. "Semiotic Phenomenology and Intercultural Communication Scholarship: Meeting the Challenge of Racial, Ethnic, and Cultural Difference." *Western Journal of Communication*, 70(4), (2006): 292–310.

————. "Semiotic Phenomenology and the 'Dialectical Approach' to Intercultural Communication: Paradigm Crisis and the Actualities of Research Practice." *Semiotica*, 2008 (169), 135–53.

Merleau-Ponty, M. *Phenomenology of Perception*, trans. Colin Smith (F. Williams & D. Guerrière, trans. revisions) New Jersey: Humanities Press 1962/1945.

————. *Signs*. Chicago: Northwestern University Press, 1964.

Mernissi, F. *Scheherazade Goes West: Different Cultures, Different Harems*. New York: Washington Square Press, 2001.

O'Sullivan, T., Hartley, J., Saunders, D, Montgomery, M., and Fiske, J. *Key Concepts in Communication and Cultural Studies*, 2nd ed. New York: Routledge, 1994.

Rodriguez, Richard. *Hunger of Memory: The Education of Richard Rodriguez*. New York: Bantam Books, 1982.

Ruesch, J., and Bateson, G. *Communication: The Social Matrix of Psychiatry*. New York: W. W. Norton & Co., 1987/1951.

Sedgwick, Eve. K. *Epistemology of the Closet*. Berkeley, Calif.: University of California Press, 1990.

Spiegelberg, Herbert. *The Phenomenological Movement: A Historical Introduction*, 3rd ed. rev. and enlarged. The Hague: Martinus Nijhoff Publishers, 1984.

Stewart, P. Jacobellis v. Ohio, 378 U.S. 184, 1964.

Van Manen, Max. *Researching Lived Experience: Human Science for an Action Sensitive Pedagogy*. Albany, N.Y.: State University of New York Press, 1990.

Index

abduction, 109

adolescence, 7, 25, 27, 29, 38, 41, 45, 53, 89, 129; and peer group xix, 18, 36, 41, 46, 48–49, 74, 89, 129, 132; and peer pressure, 40

apperception, 13, 59, 63–65

binary analogue logic, 92, 94

binary logic, xx, 38, 65, 90

body: as body image, 50, 78; and desire, 35, 38, 101; as expressive and perceptive 6, 12, 25, 50–51, 59, 61–62, 101; as lived, xvii; as memory, 131; as physical object, 9, 24, 26–27, 31–32, 65, 73, 76, 113–114 , 117

capta, 94, 104, 106, 118, 124; versus data, 94

certainty, 89–92; adequate versus apodictic, 110; reduction of, 92. *See also* information theory; uncertainty

codes, 47, 76. *See also* semiotic systems

communication theory, 92–95, 104. *See also* information theory

communicology, xvi, xvii, 5, 6, 11, 12, 13, 51, 55, 59, 72, 75–76, 97, 98, 101, 127–130

coming out, xv, 28

consciousness, xvii, 58, 76, 94, 97, 111, 114; and experience, 5, 6, 51, 57–58, 91, 101; collective, social, 44, 62–63, 53; historical, 47; of experience, 91; of self, 41

context, 1–2, 12–13, 22, 52, 59, 64, 67, 76, 81, 90, 94, 122, 131; cultural, 24; of choice versus choice of, 64, 92, 100, 104, 118; and meaning, 1, 8, 44, 68; noetic, 109–111; selection of, 65, 91, 93, 95

culture, xvi, xiv, 14, 47–49, 50, 52, 60, 68, 69, 74, 87, 88, 93, 98, 100–101, 111; as code, 22, 24, 47, 76, 108; as heteronormative, xix, 32; as preference, sensibility, 7, 117; popular, 97; U.S. American, xviii, 5, 74, 88, 129

data, 34, 91, 94, 61, 104–105, 110

description, phenomenological, 14, 102–103, 106–110, 112, 118–119

desire, xv, 2, 8, 9, 23, 39, 30, 40, 51, 101, 113. *See also* sexual, desire

discourse, 6–7, 52–53, 88, 97

embodiment, xvi, 12, 97, 99, 100, 104, 131

epochē, 14, 103, 106–107, 114, 124
experience, xvi, xviii, xx, 2, 3, 5, 6,
    11, 12, 98, 15, 18, 33, 34, 35, 38,
    45, 52, 54, 58, 72, 100, 110, 111,
    114, 115, 116, 118, 120, 129,
    130, 131, 123, 127; consciousness
    of, 91; experiencer-experiencing-
    experienced, 108, 112; immediacy
    of, 47, 55, 63, 102; as intimate,
    1, 19, 93, 124; as lived, xvi, 8–9,
    10, 14, 17, 20–21, 23, 27, 41, 46,
    59–60, 72, 95, 99, 103, 107, 109,
    117, 128, 133; of losing one's
    virginity, 122; as reversible with
    consciousness, 57, 91, 101; of
    self, 26, 29, 31. *See also* order of
    experience
expression, 10, 32–33, 39, 59, 71, 78,
    92, 106, 124, 128, 130–131; and
    perception as reversible, 51, 60, 101,
    122; social or cultural, 52

femininity, 27, 28
feminist thinking, xvi, xvii, 43, 50, 54

group network of communication,
    82–86

historicity, 13, 46, 52, 72
heteronormativity, xvi, xix, 22; and
    family, 29–30
heterosexual-homosexual binary, xx, 4,
    36–40, 48, 52, 68
heterosexuality, xx, 3–4, 28, 33, 36, 37,
    68, 82
homosexuality, xx, 3–4, 28, 32, 36, 37,
    38, 68; and desire, 78–79
human science, 5–6, 34, 91, 97, 98, 112
Husserl, Edmund, xvi, 6, 98

idealization, ideals, 9, 22–23, 54–55,
    73, 123–124, 131, 134; of sexuality,
    8, 22, 23
information theory, 14, 92–95
interpersonal: communication, 46, 79,
    83; network of communication,
    78–82, 88, 90; violence/hostility, xix,
    133

interpretation, 34, 90, 103;
    phenomenological, 14, 102–103,
    106, 109–112
intergroup network of communication,
    83–87
intrapersonal network of
    communication, 77–79, 87–88
intersexed, 24, 26, 32–33
intersubjectivity, 14, 51, 57, 71, 72, 108
intimacy, 1–2, 8–9, 19, 42, 45, 99, 124,
    127, 133–134

Jakobson, Roman, 6, 13, 58, 61
judgment, 8, 18, 33, 46, 48, 55, 88, 93

knowledge, 89, 95, 110–111, 129; in
    the body, 131; as legitimate, 3–4, 97;
    as presupposition, 4–5; as cultural,
    5, 68, 88, 123; of self, xv, 21; sexual,
    23, 33, 35–36, 45, 48

labels, 38, 68, 85; in social science, 5; in
    every day life, 84
language, 10–11, 59–60, 66, 72–73, 76,
    98, 111, 117–119, 128; diachronic
    study of, 60; objective study of,
    61, 99; synchronic study of, 61;
    paradigmatic and syntagmatic axes,
    65–67. *See also* speech spoken/
    speaking
Lanigan, Richard, xiii, 5, 6, 12, 13, 51,
    58, 59, 62, 91, 92, 94, 97, 98, 101,
    106, 107, 108, 109, 117
listening, xvii, 21, 46–47, 59, 62, 63, 65,
    98, 100, 115, 116, 118, 128, 131
love, 9, 22, 39, 54, 73, 76, 124, 131, 134

marked terms, xix, 3, 59, 64, 67–68, 88
masculinity, 19, 27–29, 36, 39, 41
maturity, 8, 10, 19, 27, 127, 130;
    sexual, 7, 35, 38, 40–41, 49, 62;
    pedagogical, xiv, xviii, 12, 20, 129
Merleau-Ponty, Maurice, 6, 45, 58, 61,
    62, 99, 107, 100, 114, 130
methodology, xix, 6, 13, 14, 98,
    101, 122, 129; as practice, 112; as
    recursive and synergistic, 14, 102–
    104, 112, 114, 122
monogamy, sexual, xviii, 29, 30, 34, 37

noema, 106, 108–111
noesis, 106, 108–111

objectivity, objective, 5, 62, 74–75, 99, 106, 134, 135
order of analysis and order of experience, 104–106, 108, 112

pedophilia, 40
peer group, xix, 2, 18, 41, 46, 74, 89
Peirce, Charles Sanders, 6, 98, 109, 111
perception, 3–6, 46–48, 51, 53, 59–60, 62, 64–65, 68, 71, 74, 78–79, 88, 89–92, 95, 101, 106, 122; erotic, 114
phenomenology, 72, 91, 97–98, 106. *See also* semiotic phenomenology
presuppositions, 3–4, 6, 12–14, 20, 23, 27, 33, 40–41, 45, 55, 71, 91, 107, 120, 127
positivism, 98, 105–106
poststructuralism, xvii

queer theory, xvii

race, racism, xvii
rationality, rational thought, 4, 97
realization, 119
reduction, phenomenological, 14, 67, 102–103, 109–112, 127
reflection, 21, 29, 44, 46, 49, 51–52, 55, 59, 72, 77–78, 90, 95, 106, 111, 113–114, 118, 119
reflexivity, 6, 50–52, 101, 111, 118
respect, 8; self, 18–20, 22; pedagogical, xvi, xviii, 19, 41, 130
Reusch, Jurgen and Bateson, Gregory, 72, 76, 77, 79, 84, 87, 95, 138
revelatory phrase, 67, 110
reversibility, 6, 51–53, 59, 101, 118

safe sex, 33
sedimentations, 45, 55, 57, 72
self-understanding, xv, 19–21, 24, 33, 46, 48–49, 90, 133
semiotics, 14, 21, 52, 57–59, 60, 71, 97, 98, 99

semiotic phenomenology xvi–xix, 6, 13–14, 51, 55, 60, 62, 97–99, 101–103, 112, 114, 122, 124, 127–130. *See also* semiotics, phenomenology
sexualities, 2, 4, 116; as communicative, 10–11; conceptualizations of, 23
sexuality: as good and/or bad, xvii, 8, 10, 15, 40, 48, 133–134; and power, 9, 43, 73, 58, 97
sexual: degradation, 6, 40; desire, xviii, 1–3, 7, 10, 22, 35, 37, 38–40, 73–74, 78–79, 82, 101, 113–114, 119–120, 134; expression, 39; fantasy, 34, 75; fulfillment, xviii, 1–2, 6–7, 10, 35, 37–39, 74–75, 113–114, 124, 134; knowledge, 5, 34, 45, 48; self-awareness, 7, 8, 38, 132; self-discovery, 3–4
silence: forced or imposed, 8, 99; and speech, 94
situatedness, human, 11, 52, 57, 59, 72, 74, 89, 94–95, 97, 106
social science, 4–5, 34–35, 91, 105
speaking subject, 61
speech-speaking and speech-spoken, 107, 130
structuralism, 13, 58, 60
structure, structures, 41, 57–60, 61, 65–66, 72, 76, 98, 82, 101, 108, 110; as constraining and enabling, 23, 58, 71, 74–75, 83; as essential, 106, 116–117, 212; meaning, 63, 73; temporal, 46, 107, 109

temporality, 13, 44, 46, 52, 55, 57, 61, 64–65, 72
trangender and/or transsexuality, xx, xix, 31–33, 48
typification, 115–117, 124

uncertainty, 92, 121
unmarked terms, 13, 59, 67–68

violence, xvii, xx, 9, 33, 52; sexual, 8, 13, 19, 40–41, 73, 133; relational, 15, 133

women's movement, 43, 52

About the Author

Jacqueline M. Martinez is associate professor of communicology at Arizona State University, where she teaches courses in semiotics, phenomenology, sexuality, and culture. Her previous book, *Phenomenology of Chicana Experience and Identity: Communication and Transformation in Praxis* (Lanham, Md.: Rowman & Littlefield, 2000), received the Outstanding Scholarship Award from the International and Intercultural Communication Division of the National Communication Association. Some of her publications appear in the *Journal of Homosexuality*, *The American Journal of Semiotics*, and *Semiotica*.

CPSIA information can be obtained at www.ICGtesting.com

263563BV00002B/7/P

9 780739 125359